DUTCH OVEN COOKBOOK

EASY-TO-FOLLOW DELICIOUS
RECIPES FOR ONE POT MEALS

Christopher Lester

A perfect dinner for me is being with people I really want to be with. It starts and stops with my company and my family.

TABLE OF CONTENTS

INTRODUCTION

IN THE SUMMERTIME, my family and I usually go hiking and camping. And one of the things I love most about it is cooking on the campfire. The best meals we make there are the ones in a **Dutch oven**. Dutch ovens come in a variety of types (brands, shapes, sizes, colors), but whichever you choose, the food made in them is, for some reason, **tastier than the same food cooked in a regular old pot.**

The great news is that you don't have to go hiking to cook this way! You can make all of these recipes right at home in your kitchen.

My family really loves getting together at the table and brightening long chilly winter evenings with **heartwarming meals cooked in a Dutch oven**, whether that be chicken, some mutton stew, or our favorite ragout.

Follow along with me to learn six ways of cooking delicious foods in a Dutch oven.

WHAT DUTCH OVENS ARE?

Cold season is easier to live through when you have some nice, delicious comfort foods. It hasn't been long since I was skeptically listening to enthusiasts of **Dutch ovens**. However, I am constantly learning something new, and now it's my turn to tell you about the advantages of this miraculous pot. To be honest, I wouldn't know how to go without one anymore.

❖ **So, what is a "Dutch oven?"** It is a thick-walled cooking pot with a tight-fitting lid. Dutch ovens can be made of seasoned or enameled cast iron, cast aluminum, or ceramic.

They all are extremely durable and resistant to high temperatures, and thanks to the various colors and designs in which they are produced, a Dutch oven can easily fit into any kitchen décor / design.

Actually, people have been using different kinds of pots for cooking since ancient times. But it was only at the beginning of the 1700s that the ancestors of modern Dutch ovens—the first cast iron cooking pots created with so-called **"Dutch technology"**—were produced. You won't believe this, but in the Netherlands themselves, the first models of Dutch ovens were not introduced until the late 1800s.

Today you can choose the size of your Dutch oven (usually 8″ to 16″ in diameter). There are dedicated models for camping: with a long handle and long stands, as well as smaller ones that can easily fit in any home kitchen. **Thanks to their design, Dutch ovens heat up evenly and can maintain their temperature for a long time.** All of that makes them great for both professional and home use.

How Dutch Ovens Work?

A Dutch oven is great for cooking dishes that need high (or low) temperature, evenly allocated, and with long-term heating maintained.

Use a Dutch oven if you need to:

- **Fry**

- **Roast**

- **Stew**

- **Braise**

- **Boil**

- **Bake**

A Dutch oven is particularly convenient if you are cooking a dish that requires combining several cooking techniques. For example, you can first fry something up on the stove, and then add other ingredients and put the stew in the oven. Cooking a complex meal in one vessel is very simple and convenient. In the end, you only need to wash one pot.

I prefer to use a Dutch oven to make a roasted chicken, beef stews, and ragouts. As a matter of fact, a Dutch oven is a cooking vessel that can replace many others. Use it to cook countless dishes, make soups, fry and roast meat, bake a cobbler, or even cook a pizza.

This ultimate device helps cook tasty and healthy food for the whole family. Home cooking becomes so much easier when you can do everything in a single pot!

Benefits of a Dutch Oven

Professional and amateur chefs alike love Dutch ovens, and they definitely have a good reason. Let's take a look at their main advantages:

1. They are made of **very durable and damage-proof materials**, and thus may serve you a lifetime.
2. It **warms up evenly**, and the heat is allocated all over the surface and maintained for a long time.
3. They are deep, and thus, all the **splash and spatter stays inside**; moreover, you get some additional vessel volume that doesn't take extra space on the stove.
4. You can use them both on the **stove and in the oven.**
5. They come in **various sizes, as well as attractive** and colorful designs, and thus will complement most any kitchen interior. Plus, the enamel coating does not tarnish or wear out.
6. They require **minimal maintenance** and can be washed in the dishwasher.
7. Dutch ovens are truly universal! You can use them to **stew, boil, fry, roast, bake**, etc.

Dutch Oven Care and Maintenance

Manufacturers have done their best to make Dutch ovens as durable as possible, but if you want to maximize the life of your reliable helper, you should follow some rules:

1. **Do not use sharp utensils** that could damage the enamel coating.
2. **Use long tongs with silicone tips.** This will protect your hands from hot drops and the Dutch oven from scratches.

3. Always **hold the pot with both hands**. A full Dutch oven is really heavy, and you need to be careful with it.

4. Let your Dutch oven **cool down** before you put it in cold water.

Stewed Beef

I sincerely love cooking beef stew in my Dutch oven!

Beef is easily digested and provides us with necessary proteins and amino acids. It is particularly recommended for patients recovering after a surgery. You can cook it in different ways: fry, boil, bake, marinate, grill, smoke, and many more. Beef meals—like Beef Stroganoff, English roast beef, American filet mignon, and Mexican chili con carne—have long conquered the world.

But it's hard to imagine a healthier and lower fat meat meal than stewed beef. No wonder it has been loved ever since ancient Roman and Greek times, where it was one of the popular noble specialties. Its different versions have reached our times as British cannelon, French rillettes, and Russian tushonka.

You can season stewed beef with **marjoram, thyme, a bay leaf, pepper**, or any other of many herbs and spices, and then serve with a sauce sprinkled with herbs and complemented with **red wine**, along with numerous side dishes including **cereals, pasta, or vegetables**.

By the way, good fresh beef has a light milk aroma, and it is better not to freeze it if you want to save the flavor.

Chicken in a Dutch Oven

My second favorite dish from the Dutch oven is chicken.

Chicken is rather easy to raise, and depending on the breed, they can reach the weight of from 1.5 to 5 kg (3 – 11 lb). This makes them a popular kind of domestic fowl that people have been breeding for centuries.

Chicken meat is a dietary product **rich in proteins and amino acids**, but its white meat (breast) contains less fat than dark meat (leg quarters). It is advised for people suffering from illnesses such as gout, polyarthritis, diabetes, and ulcers.

Frozen chicken can be stored in the freezer for 6-9 months. It should be defrosted in the fridge (*not* at room temperature!) To prepare a chicken for cooking, you need to rinse it with water and then, if necessary, cut it into pieces.

It is better not to overcook the chicken meat, and to eat it immediately after cooking. If you are striving for some rich broth, put the meat in cold water, and to get some savory boiled meat, place the chicken into boiling water.

In this book, you will find many chicken-based recipes. This meat is nice **to boil, fry, stew, and bake**. It is easy to prepare and can be combined with other types of meat.

TASTY POULTRY DISHES

Chicken Cacciatore

This chicken recipe is really special for several reasons. For one thing, it makes for a filling meal. Also, all the ingredients come out nicely seared and crunchy as you fry each of them separately.

INGREDIENTS:

- 4 – 4½ pounds chicken, bone-in, skin-on, and trimmed
- salt and black pepper, to taste

- 4 tablespoons extra-virgin olive oil
- 1 cup onion, diced
- 4 garlic cloves, minced
- 8 ounces mushrooms, sliced

- 2 red or yellow bell peppers, diced
- ½ cup dry red wine
- 2 tablespoons capers
- 2 teaspoons dried oregano
- 2 teaspoons dried rosemary
- 28 ounces canned diced tomatoes with liquid
- 1 cup chicken broth
- 1 bay leaf

OPTIONAL FOR GARNISH:

- chopped fresh parsley
- grated parmesan cheese

DIRECTIONS:

1. Season chicken pieces with salt and pepper.
2. Heat a Dutch oven over medium heat. Pour in olive oil and heat until rippling.
3. Working in batches, add chicken pieces, cooking 3 minutes on each side until slightly brown. Remove chicken from Dutch oven; set chicken aside.
4. Add diced onion and pepper to the pan and saute for 5 minutes.
5. Toss in mushrooms and continue to saute for another 3 minutes.
6. Place all vegetables to one side of the pan. Then add minced garlic, capers, oregano, and rosemary; stir constantly for 1 minute.
7. Stir in wine and cook for 3 minutes, scraping up any brown bits from the bottom of the pan.
8. Add in diced tomatoes (with liquid), chicken broth, and bay leaf; bring to a low boil. Add salt and pepper to taste.
9. Add browned chicken pieces into the sauce; bring to a simmer, and then reduce heat to low. Cover and cook for a minimum of 45 minutes up to 2 hours.
10. Garnish with chopped fresh parsley or grated parmesan cheese, as desired.
11. Serve warm over mashed potatoes, roasted vegetables, pasta, or rice.

NUTRITIONAL INFORMATION (PER SERVING)

Calories 406

Total Fat 12.2g, Saturated Fat 2.6g, Cholesterol 157mg, Sodium 387mg, Total Carbohydrate 7.8g, Dietary Fiber 1.7g, Total Sugars 4g, Protein 61.5g, Vitamin D 82mcg, Calcium 56mg, Iron 3mg, Potassium 561mg

Korean Fried Chicken

Korean-style crunchy chicken is an ideal recipe for those who love hot and spicy hints and a crispy crust, emphasizing the tenderness of the chicken meat.

INGREDIENTS:

- 2 cups vegetable oil
- 2 pounds chicken wings
- Kosher salt and freshly ground black pepper, to taste
- ½ cup soy sauce
- ¼ cup plus 2 tablespoons sugar

DIRECTIONS:

1. Heat vegetable oil in a Dutch oven over medium-high heat, about 300°F.

2. Season chicken wings with salt and pepper.

3. Working in batches, add 5 to 6 pieces of chicken wings to the Dutch oven and fry until light brown, about 2 – 3 minutes. Transfer to a paper towel-lined plate.

4. Increase oil temperature to 350°F. Add the chicken wings to the Dutch oven again and cook until golden brown and crispy, about 2 minutes on each side. Transfer to a paper towel-lined plate.

5. Heat soy sauce and sugar in a small saucepan over medium-high heat. Bring to a boil. Reduce heat to low and simmer, stirring occasionally for about 2-3 minutes until sauce has thickened.

6. Toss chicken wings in soy sauce glaze and serve immediately.

NUTRITIONAL INFORMATION (PER SERVING)

Calories 1458

Total Fat 125.8g, Saturated Fat 26g, Cholesterol 202mg, Sodium 2031mg, Total Carbohydrate 15g, Dietary Fiber 0.3g, Total Sugars 13g, Protein 67.6g, Vitamin D 0mcg, Calcium 40mg, Iron 3mg, Potassium 621mg

Sweet and Savory Baked Apples and Chicken

I believe that chicken meat is so versatile. You can cook it in a broad variety of ways, add diverse stuffing and seasonings, and it will always be delicious.

INGREDIENTS:

- 1 Gala or Pink Lady apple, diced
- 1 sweet yellow onion, diced
- 2 Roma tomatoes, sliced
- 2 chicken breasts, cut into chunks
- dash of salt

- dash of pepper
- dash of ginger powder
- ½ cup raisins
- cinnamon

DIRECTIONS:

1. Preheat oven to 375°F.

2. Mix apple, onions, and tomatoes in a bowl. Using 2/3 of this mixture, make a base layer in a Dutch oven. Set aside 1/3 of the mixture for later.

3. Season with salt, pepper, and ginger.

4. Add a sprinkle of cinnamon over the base layer.

5. Place the chunks of chicken over the base layer.

6. Place the remaining mixture of apple, tomato, and onion to make a top layer.

7. Sprinkle with a fair amount of cinnamon, then cover with raisins.

8. Place Dutch oven into the preheated oven. Cook for about 45-60 minutes.

9. Remove from oven. Do NOT lift the lid. Allow sitting for about 15 minutes before serving, until the juices disperse and settle.

NUTRITIONAL INFORMATION (PER SERVING)

Calories 470

Total Fat 11g, Saturated Fat 2.9g, Cholesterol 125mg, Sodium 207mg, Total Carbohydrate 48.2g, Dietary Fiber 8.2g, Total Sugars 37.4 g, Protein 42.4g, Vitamin D 0mcg, Calcium 89mg, Iron 3 mg, Potassium 733 mg

Brads Chicken Cutlets & Gnocchi with Mushroom Tarragon Cream Sauce

Italian gnocchi has long been popular far beyond Italy. Different sauces and seasonings let you change the taste of it, creating, even more, new, tasty, and filling meals. We suggest you try this recipe of gnocchi in mushroom sauce with chicken and tarragon.

INGREDIENTS:

- 3 large chicken breasts, filleted and pounded flat
- flour for dredging
- 1 teaspoon lemon pepper
- 1 teaspoon garlic powder
- 1 teaspoon white pepper
- 1 teaspoon ground mustard
- 2 eggs, beaten
- crumbs

FOR THE SAUCE:

- 1 large shallot, finely chopped
- 8 large crimini mushrooms, thinly sliced
- 2 tablespoons butter

- 1 tablespoon garlic, minced
- 6 springs fresh tarragon, minced
- 1 quart whipping cream
- 2 tablespoons granulated chicken broth
- 1 teaspoon white pepper
- 2 tablespoons mustard
- 1 cup Parmesan, shredded
- 1/8 cup cornstarch, mixed with cold water for thickening
- gnocchi

DIRECTIONS:

1. Set up a breading station by mixing flour and all the seasonings. Place beaten eggs in one bowl, and panko crumbs in another.

2. Boil a large pot of heavily salted water. Drop in gnocchi; boil for 2 minutes until they float to the top. Strain, rinse and set aside.

3. For the sauce, melt butter in a Dutch oven. Add shallots and mushrooms, then sauté until they start to caramelize.

4. Add garlic and tarragon. Sauté for 2 more minutes.

5. Add the rest of sauce ingredients except for the corn starch and cheese. Bring to a simmer.

6. At the same time, heat oil in a pan.

7. Dredge chicken in seasoned flour, then in eggs, then in crumbs. Fry in a pan until golden brown. Drain on paper towels.

8. When the sauce simmers, add gnocchi and cheese, then let it simmer again until sauce slightly thickens. Use starch to bring to desired consistency.

9. Plate gnocchi. Serve chicken on top. If desired, garnish with more cheese and a small sprig of tarragon.

10. Serve and enjoy.

NUTRITIONAL INFORMATION (PER SERVING)

Calories 850

Total Fat 59.8 g, Saturated Fat 33.4g, Cholesterol 338 mg, Sodium 777 mg, Total Carbohydrate 30.3 g, Dietary Fiber 1.8 g, Total Sugars 2.2 g, Protein 48.3 g, Vitamin D 12 mcg, Calcium 424 mg, Iron 4 mg, Potassium 729 mg

Dutch Oven Sprite Chicken

Delicious chicken, potatoes, and carrots cooked in a Dutch oven... the flavor of this meal is incredible. Enjoy at home, or at a campout!

INGREDIENTS:

- ½ pound bacon, cut into bite-size pieces
- 3 large boneless skinless chicken breasts, cut into 1-inch cubes
- ½ tablespoon seasoning salt
- ½ cup all-purpose flour
- 1 yellow onion, chopped
- 2 pounds red potatoes, cut into 1-inch cubes
- 1 pound carrots, cut into 2-inch pieces
- 6 ounces Sprite (or any lemon-lime soda)

DIRECTIONS:

1. Preheat oven to 350°F.

2. Fry bacon in a Dutch oven on Camp Chef or stove top until crisp. Remove bacon pieces with a slotted spoon, leaving grease. Set bacon aside.

3. Combine seasoning salt and flour in a large gallon plastic bag. Add chicken to flour mixture and shake to coat.

4. Add coated chicken pieces to Dutch oven and brown in bacon grease.

5. Remove chicken and set aside.

6. Add the following ingredients to your Dutch oven, in this order: onions, then potatoes, then carrots, then chicken, and then the previously set aside bacon. Pour Sprite all over the top. Cover with lid.

7. Bake at 350°F for 1 hour. Carefully remove from oven. Remove lid and let stand 5 minutes before serving.

NOTE: If cooking at a campsite, follow directions 2 – 5 above. When ready to cook, cover with a lid and place Dutch oven on hot coals. Cook for 45 minutes to 1 hour (or until chicken is cooked through and vegetables are tender).

NUTRITIONAL INFORMATION (PER SERVING)

Calories 398
Total Fat 16 g, Saturated Fat 5 g, Cholesterol 78 mg, Sodium 1188 mg, Total Carbohydrate 33.5g, Dietary Fiber 3.8 g, Total Sugars 6.8 g, Protein 29.3g, Vitamin D0 mcg, Calcium 46mg, Iron 2 mg, Potassium 1014 mg

Juicy Chicken with Vegetables

Vegetables add new bright flavor to the ordinary chicken. The meat is soaked with vegetable juices and becomes amazingly tender and fragrant.

INGREDIENTS:

- 1 chicken
- 4 potatoes
- 2 carrots
- 2 onions
- 1 cup mushrooms
- some greens to taste
- salt and pepper to taste
- 1 garlic clove
- 2 tablespoons butter
- 2 tablespoons vegetable oil
- ½ cup water

DIRECTIONS:

1. Preheat oven to 360°F.

2. Take the whole chicken and cut it into small pieces.

3. Rub chicken with salt, pepper, and garlic.

4. Melt the butter in a pan and lightly fry all the chicken pieces until golden brown.

5. Peel all the vegetables, then cut the potatoes into large pieces, cut onions and mushrooms into small cubes, and grate the carrots.

6. Fry onion, carrots, and mushrooms in vegetable oil.

7. Put chicken, roasted vegetables and potatoes into the Dutch oven. Cover with water.

8. Place lid on Dutch oven and put in preheated oven for 45 minutes.

9. Remove from oven, sprinkle with finely chopped herbs, and serve.

NUTRITIONAL INFORMATION (PER SERVING)

Calories 308

Total Fat 16 g, Saturated Fat 5.3 g, Cholesterol 37mg, Sodium 161mg, Total Carbohydrate 32g, Dietary Fiber 4.9 g, Total Sugars 4.4g, Protein 10.1g, Vitamin D 45mcg, Calcium 37mg, Iron 2 mg, Potassium 784 mg

Chicken in a Brazier

CHICKEN IN
A BRAZIER

COOKING TIME: 1 ½ HOURS
SERVING: 4

Stewed chicken with potatoes is an easy and hearty dish. Meat juice is absorbed by vegetables, and it turns out very tasty. It is also a very fast, yet delicious, recipe for chicken with potatoes. You can cook it any time, for lunch or dinner.

INGREDIENTS:

- 1 chicken (50 – 60 ounces)
- 2 teaspoons salt
- ½ teaspoon freshly ground black pepper
- 1 teaspoon red ground pepper
- 1 garlic clove
- 3 onions, finely chopped

- 2 carrots, cut into strips
- 3 potatoes, peeled and cut into quarters
- 2 cups mushrooms
- 4 tablespoons butter
- 2 tablespoons vegetable oil
- ½ cup broth (or water)
- 2 tablespoons parsley, finely chopped

DIRECTIONS:

1. Preheat oven to 380°F.

2. Cut the chicken into pieces, wash it, dry with a kitchen towel, and rub pieces with salt, black pepper, garlic, and red pepper.

3. Melt the butter in a frying pan and fry the chicken in it.

4. In another frying pan fry slightly the onions, mushrooms, carrots, and potatoes.

5. Put the vegetables and chicken in a Dutch oven (or brazier, deep form), add broth or water, cover, and place in preheated oven for 1 hour.

6. Take off the lid, sprinkle with parsley, and serve.

NUTRITIONAL INFORMATION (PER SERVING)

Calories 941

Total Fat 32.8 g, Saturated Fat 8.7 g, Cholesterol 389 mg, Sodium 1660 mg, Total Carbohydrate 30.6 g, Dietary Fiber 5.3 g, Total Sugars 4.5 g, Protein 123.7g, Vitamin D 134mcg, Calcium 64 mg, Iron 4 mg, Potassium 2990 mg

Easy Grecian Dutch Oven Chicken

This is an extremely simple Grecian Chicken recipe that is easy to make but does not compromise on the awesome flavor coming from the mixture of lemon and Italian spices

INGREDIENTS:

- 3 ½ pounds whole chicken
- 1-2 pats butter
- Salt as needed
- Pepper as needed

- 1 tablespoon oregano, dried
- ¾ cup garlic, peeled
- 2 lemons, sliced into thin rounds

DIRECTIONS:

1. Carefully preheat your oven to 375° F.

2. Take the chicken and stuff half of one lemon and about 5-8 cloves of garlic into its cavity. This will ensure that the chicken stays moist throughout the process.

3. Season the chicken with salt and pepper according to your taste.

4. Transfer prepared chicken to Dutch oven and add remaining lemon slices and garlic cloves, sprinkle oregano on top.

5. Add 1-2 pats of butter if you want the chicken to be crispier.

6. Place lid and let it cook for about 1 and ½ hours, making sure to keep checking the temperature at an internal of 10 minutes after the first hour.

7. Once the internal temperature of the thickest part of the chicken reaches 160°F, remove the heat and let the chicken stand for 10 minutes.

8. Remove from the pan and carve.

9. Serve and enjoy!

NUTRITIONAL INFORMATION (PER SERVING):

Calories: 548

Total Fat: 21.2 g, Saturated Fat: 6.3 g, Cholesterol: 239 mg, Sodium: 268 mg, Total Carbohydrate: 7.9 g, Dietary Fiber: 1.2 g, Total Sugar: 0.7 g, Protein: 77.9 g, Vitamin D: 1 mcg, Calcium: 88 mg , Iron: 4 mg, Potassium 751mg

Simple Lemon and Garlic Whole Chicken Roast

LEMON GARLIC WHOLE CHICKEN ROAST

PREP TIME: 15 MIN
COOKING TIME: 1 ½ HOURS
SERVING: 4

Juicy and crusty chicken with a plenty of butter, garlic, rosemary, and lemon. Just put it in the oven!

INGREDIENTS:

- 1 whole chicken
- ½ stick butter or ghee
- 2 large onions, thickly sliced
- 4 sprigs rosemary, 3 finely chopped and 1 reserved
- 2 lemons, halved
- 5 cloves garlic, 3 minced and 2 cups in half
- Salt and pepper as needed

DIRECTIONS:

1. Pre-heat your Dutch oven to 475°F.

2. Take a small sized oven proof bowl and melt butter in your oven.

3. Add minced garlic, lemon zest, rosemary, lemons and season accordingly with salt and pepper.

4. Slice onions thickly and carefully arrange them at the bottom of your cast iron Dutch oven.

5. Reserve the end scraps for later use.

6. Prepare your whole chicken by removing the giblets from cavity.

7. Rinse the chicken thoroughly and pat it dry.

8. Season the cavity with salt and pepper according to your taste.

9. Cut lemons in half, making sure to reserve the juice. Keep the rinds as well.

10. By now your butter mixture should be hard, so use your hand to slather the butter all over the chicken roast.

11. Transfer the prepared chicken on top of your sliced onions.

12. Stuff the cavity of the chicken with lemon rinds, remaining garlic, rosemary sprigs, onion scraps.

13. Use kitchen twine to carefully tie the legs of a chicken.

14. Pour reserve lemon juice on top of the chicken.

15. Roast the chicken for 15 minutes at 475°F, lower down the heat to 350°F and roast for 20 minutes per pound (if your chicken roast is 2 pounds, then cook time will go for 40 minutes).

16. While the chicken cooks, make sure to baste the chicken for further taste (the cooking should be done uncovered unless you are unable to generate enough heat).

17. Once cooking is complete, let the chicken cool and carve.

18. Serve and enjoy!

NUTRITIONAL INFORMATION (PER SERVING):

Calories: 382

Total Fat: 20g, Saturated Fat: 9g, Cholesterol: 139 mg, Sodium: 230mg, Total Carbohydrate: 11.8g, Dietary Fiber: 3g, Total Sugar: 5g, Protein: 37g, Vitamin D: 8 mcg, Calcium:68mg, Iron: 2mg, Potassium 477mg,

Hearty Braised Chicken Thigh's Dipped In Tomato Sauce

Should you have a thing for Mediterranean cuisine, this is easy to make, healthy and filling dish is a great option to diversify your everyday menu.

INGREDIENTS:

- 6 chicken thighs
- 6 chicken legs
- 4 bay leaves, dried
- 2 sticks cinnamon
- 1 can (28 ounces) whole tomatoes, peeled
- 6 garlic cloves, peeled and halved
- 1 large knob of ginger, peeled and grated
- 4 tablespoons olive oil
- Salt as needed
- 1 teaspoon whole cumin seeds
- 2 teaspoons chili flakes
- 1 large white onion, peeled and halved, thinly sliced
- Water, as needed

DIRECTIONS:

1. Take a large skillet and place it over high heat.

2. Add olive oil and heat it up.

3. Add chicken thigh and legs on a tray (arranging them in a single layer and season according to your taste).

4. Once the oil begins to smoke, add chicken to the oil (make sure to not overcrowd the skillet).

5. Cook the chicken for 3-5 minutes per side. Use metal tongs to turn the pieces.

6. Transfer chicken back to the tray and keep it on the side.

7. Add cumin seeds and chili flakes to the same skillet and toast for 10-15 seconds.

8. Add onions, ginger, garlic and stir well.

9. Season with salt, then add cinnamon, tomatoes and bay leaf.

10. Stir well and let the mixture cook for about 10 minutes to allow the flavors to seep in.

11. Add chicken back to the pan and keep it on low heat, cook for 30-45 minutes.

12. Once the chicken is thoroughly cooked, discard bay leaves and cinnamon sticks.

13. Taste and season with more salt if needed.

NUTRITIONAL INFORMATION (PER SERVING):

Calories: 376

Total Fat: 18 g, Saturated Fat: 3.7 g, Cholesterol: 140 mg, Sodium: 157 mg, Total Carbohydrate: 4 g, Dietary Fiber: 0.9 g, Total Sugar: 0.9 g, Protein:46 g, Vitamin D: 0 mcg, Calcium: 43 mg, Iron: 2 mg, Potassium 432mg,

FAVORITE MEAT DISHES

Juicy Curried Meatballs

Meatballs in curry will perfectly match almost any common side dish: rice, mashed potatoes, couscous, whatsoever. And, what is even more important, they are really delicious! Who could have thought that such a straightforward meal can be so good!

INGREDIENTS:

FOR MEAT BALLS

- 2 pounds ground beef, 20% fat
- 2 teaspoons salt

- 3 tablespoons sweet/plain yogurt
- 1 large egg, beaten
- ½ teaspoon cayenne pepper/paprika
- ½ teaspoon ground cumin

- 1 teaspoon ground coriander

- 1 tablespoon Garam Masala

- 1 tablespoon fresh lemon juice

- 6 garlic cloves

- 1 piece 1-inch garlic, peeled and chopped

- 2 jalapenos, seeded

- 6 scallions, cut into 1-inch pieces

- Olive oil as needed

FOR CURRY SAUCE

- Cilantro leaves with tender stems (for serving)

- ½ teaspoon paprika

- 1 tablespoon fresh lemon juice

- 1 tablespoon kosher salt

- 1 bay leaf

- 1 can (14.5 ounces) crushed tomatoes

- 1 teaspoon black peppercorns

- 3 tablespoons ground coriander

- 4 teaspoons ground cumin

- 4 teaspoons ground turmeric

- 4 teaspoons curry powder

- 3 dried chili peppers

- 1 and 1/2 inch piece ginger, peeled and chopped

- ¼ cup olive oil

- 4 medium onions, chopped

DIRECTIONS:
FOR MEAT BALLS

1. Pre-heat your oven to a temperature of 400°F.

2. Take a rimmed baking sheet and lightly brush it with oil.

3. Take your food processor and add scallions, garlic, ginger, lemon juice, garam masala, jalapenos, coriander, cumin, and cayenne.

4. Blend well until smooth and pureed.

5. Transfer the whole mixture to a bowl and add egg, beef, yogurt, and salt.

6. Mix well using your hand until everything incorporates well.

7. Portion the mixture into golf ball sized portions and transfer them to your baking sheet (maintaining a distance of 1 inch between the balls).

8. Drizzle balls with more oil and bake for 20-25 minutes.

FOR CURRY SAUCE

1. Add oil to your Dutch oven and heat it up.

2. Add onions, ginger, garlic and cook for 8-10 minutes until translucent.

3. Add chilies, cumin, curry powder, turmeric, coriander, and peppercorns.

4. Cook for 2 minutes until the mixture is fragrant.

5. Add tomatoes, and keep stirring to scrap the bottom.

6. Bring the mixture to a boil and add bay leaf, 1 tablespoon salt and 2 cups of water.

7. Return the mix to boil again.

8. Lower down heat and let it simmer for 25-30 minutes, in order to allow the flavors to seep in.

9. Let it cool and transfer to a blender.

10. Blend until smooth.

11. Wipe out any remaining bits and transfer curry sauce back to the pot.

12. Stir in lemon juice and cayenne.

13. Season with salt.

14. Carefully introduce the baked meatballs to the sauce and bring to a simmer.

15. Cook for 10-15 minutes and serve with topped cilantro.

NUTRITIONAL INFORMATION (PER SERVING):

Calories: 375

Total Fat: 17 g, Saturated Fat: 5 g, Cholesterol: 125 mg, Sodium: 165 mg, Total Carbohydrate: 16g, Dietary Fiber: 4.4g, Total Sugar: 6g, Protein: 38g, Vitamin D: 38mcg, Calcium: 95mg, Iron: 25 mg, Potassium 74 mg

Amazing Flat Iron Rouladen

AMAZING
FLAT IRON
ROULADEN

PREP TIME: 45 MIN
COOKING TIME: 1 ½ HOURS
SERVING: 4

Bacon strips will add some smokie flavor to the steak, and the grease they contain will help to keep the meet toothsome. You can sear both sides of your bacon wrapped steaks on a heated skillet and then put them in the oven, or simply grill them — just make sure that bacon strips shrink and tightly wrap around the meat to keep the juice in.

INGREDIENTS:

- 1 (1 and ½ pounds) piece of flatiron steak, butterflied, cut into 4 equal pieces and pounded to ¼ inch thickness
- 6 bacon slices, cut into lardons
- 1 can (14 and ½ ounces) tomatoes, diced
- ¼ cup red wine

- 2 cloves garlic, minced
- 1 celery stalk, chopped
- 1 large carrot, chopped
- 2 tablespoons olive oil
- 2 tablespoons pickled relish
- 2 tablespoons Dijon mustard
- 1 and ½ large yellow onion, diced
- Salt and pepper to taste

DIRECTIONS:

1. Pre-heat your oven to a temperature of 325°F.

2. Take a small sized sauté pan and place it over medium-low heat.

3. Add bacon until it has rendered its fat. Keep it on the side.

4. Season your steaks with salt and pepper according to your taste and lay them flat on a large-sized cutting board.

5. Brush the top with mustard and coat it well.

6. Take a small bowl and add half of onion and pickle relish, alongside reserved bacon.

7. Season with salt and spread the onion mix over your meat.

8. Start from the short end, and roll up your meat, similar to a jelly roll. Secure with kitchen twine.

9. Take your Dutch oven and place it over medium-high heat.

10. Add meat and brown all sides. Remove meat from pan and keep it on the side.

11. Add rest of the onion, celery, carrot and cook for 5 minutes.

12. Add garlic and cook for 1 minute more.

13. Deglaze pan with wine and add the canned tomatoes, alongside any juices.

14. Gently re-introduce the meat to the pan and bring the mix to a simmer.

15. Cover and let it bake for 90 minutes.

16. Make sure to turn the meat halfway through.

NUTRITIONAL INFORMATION (PER SERVING):

Calories: 473

Total Fat: 27 g, Saturated Fat: 9 g, Cholesterol: 79 mg, Sodium: 935 mg, Total Carbohydrate: 15g, Dietary Fiber: 3.3 g, Total Sugar: 9g, Protein: 37g, Vitamin D: 0 mcg, Calcium: 46mg, Iron: 4 mg, Potassium 886 mg,

Authentic and Really Spicy Firehouse Chili

Meat and bean stews are eaten all over the world. It is difficult to say where it has originated: Mexican chili con carne, Jewish cholent, Brazilian feijoada, French cassoulet and many other traditional meals follows the similar recipe. Whoever made it first, braised beef in a vegetable sauce with canned red beans is loved by numerous families all over the world. It is a delicious and filling dinner, which will please your taste buds and provide your body with some useful proteins.

INGREDIENTS:

- 4 pounds (90%) lean ground beef
- 1 teaspoon oregano, dried
- 4 garlic cloves, minced
- 2 tablespoons ground cumin
- 2 tablespoons ground coriander
- 3 tablespoons chili powder
- 1 can (14 and ½ ounces each) beef broth
- 3 cans (14 and ½ ounces each) stewed tomatoes, diced
- 4 cans (16 ounces each) kidney beans, rinsed and drained

- 1 medium green pepper, chopped
- 2 medium onions, chopped
- 2 tablespoons olive oil

DIRECTIONS:

1. Heat up olive oil over medium heat in your Dutch oven.

2. Add beef in batches and brown them, making sure to crumble the meat in the process until they are no longer pink.

3. Drain any excess oil and keep the meat on the side.

4. Add onions, green pepper, cook until fragrant and shows a nice soft texture.

5. Re-introduce the meat to the oven and stir in remaining ingredients.

6. Bring the mix to a boil and lower heat, simmer (covered) for about 1 and ½ hours until thoroughly cooked and the flavors have blended.

7. Enjoy!

NUTRITIONAL INFORMATION (PER SERVING):

Calories: 443

Total Fat: 27 g, Saturated Fat: 12 g, Cholesterol: 107 mg, Sodium: 499 mg, Total Carbohydrate: 15 g, Dietary Fiber: 2 g, Total Sugar: 3 g, Protein: 27 g, Vitamin D: 0 mcg, Calcium: 62 mg, Iron: 4 mg, Potassium 565 mg

Original Dutch Oven Beef Roast

ORIGINAL
DUTCH
OVEN BEEF
ROAST

PREP TIME: 25 MIN
COOKING TIME: 2 HOURS
SERVING: 4

When cooking beef it is often extremely difficult to make it tender, but not if you are making a beef and vegetable pot roast. This is the dish that comes out so well that it deserves nothing but superlatives: the tastiest and the most tender possible! And what a sauce! When you are new to cooking there may be some danger tricky moments but once you know about them it is easy to make a lush and delicious meal!

INGREDIENTS:

- 4-5 pounds beef roast, bottom round
- Cooking fat such as butter or ghee
- Fresh thyme sprigs
- 2 bay leaves
- 2 cups beef stock
- ½ cup red wine, optional

- 1 tablespoon tomato paste
- 3 cloves garlic, minced
- 2 onions, quartered
- 1 celeriac, diced
- 4 sweet potatoes, cut up into chunks
- 3 carrots, peeled and sliced
- Salt and pepper as needed

DIRECTIONS:

1. Pre-heat your oven to a temperature of 350°F.

2. Season your beef generously with salt and pepper.

3. Take your Dutch oven and place it over medium-high heat.

4. Add butter/ghee and let it melt.

5. Add your roast and brown all sides, for about 1-2 minutes each side.

6. Add garlic, onion, tomato paste and cook for 2-3 minutes.

7. Add wine if you are using and scrap the bottom of your pan.

8. Lower heat and let it simmer until halved.

9. Add remaining vegetables, thyme, stock and bay leaves.

10. Bring the mix to a simmer (covered).

11. Transfer to oven and roast in the oven for about 2 hours until the thickest part of the meat reaches 145°F.

12. Let it cool, carve and enjoy!

NUTRITIONAL INFORMATION (PER SERVING):

Calories: 1460

Total Fat: 47 g, Saturated Fat: 16 g, Cholesterol: 544 mg, Sodium: 890 mg, Total Carbohydrate: 57 g, Dietary Fiber: 10 g, Total Sugar: 7 g, Protein:184 g, Vitamin D: 0 mcg, Calcium:121 mg, Iron: 22 mg, Potassium 3461mg

Very Creamy Bacon And Cheese Potato Soup

An elegant and extremely creamy potato soup that is oozing a sense of hearty and cheesy flavors! You are going to simply fall for it.

INGREDIENTS:

- 6 piece bacon slices
- ¼ teaspoon pepper
- 1 teaspoon salt
- 1 tablespoons fresh chives, chopped
- ¼ cup flour
- 1 cup cheddar cheese, shredded

- 2 cups water
- 2 cups whole milk
- 1 onion, chopped
- 10 garlic cloves, minced
- 2 pounds large russet potatoes, peeled and cut up into 1/2 inch pieces
- 1 whole onion, chopped

DIRECTIONS:

1. Heat up your large sized Dutch oven over medium heat.

2. Add bacon and cook for about 10-15 minutes until crispy.

3. Transfer to a paper towel and drain excess grease.

4. Once cooled, crumble into small pieces.

5. Add onions to your pot alongside bacon grease.

6. Cook for about 5 minutes until tender, making sure to stir from time to time.

7. Add flour and remaining ingredients, stir cook for 3 minutes.

8. Add water and stir until everything is mixed well.

9. Add milk and stir, bring the mix to a boil over high heat.

10. Lower down heat to medium-low and let the mixture simmer for about 15 minutes.

11. Make sure to keep stirring it in order to prevent the potatoes from burning.

12. Once done, serve in bowls with a topping of bacon crumbles, chopped chives, and cheddar.

13. Enjoy!

NUTRITIONAL INFORMATION (PER SERVING):

Calories: 1549

Total Fat: 25 g, Saturated Fat: 12 g, Cholesterol: 73 mg, Sodium: 1484 mg, Total Carbohydrate: 53 g, Dietary Fiber:7 g, Total Sugar: 10 g, Protein:27 g, Vitamin D: 52 mcg, Calcium: 391 mg, Iron: 2 mg, Potassium: 1379mg

Most Delicious Single Pot Lasagna

DELICIOUS SINGLE POT LASAGNA

PREP TIME: 10 MIN
COOKING TIME: 70 MIN
SERVING: 4

Meat lasagna is a truly delicious and filling Italian dish, and, actually, it is much easier to cook than it seems. This pasta bake layered with minced meat will definitely catch the fancy of you and your family! And the tomato sauce will saturate the dish with an intense tomato taste and savory flavors.

INGREDIENTS:

- 6-8 slices bacon cut up into small pieces
- 3 carrots, minced
- 3 shallots, minced
- 1 pound beef, ground
- Salt and pepper to taste

- 1 jar (25 ounces) tomato basil sauce
- ½ cup dry red wine
- 4 ounces cream cheese
- 6-8 ounces fresh mozzarella cheese
- 4 ounces whole wheat no-boil lasagna noodles
- Basil and parmesan cheese, for topping

DIRECTIONS:

1. Pre-heat your oven to a temperature of 350°F.

2. Take a large ovenproof skillet and brown your bacon until it is crispy.

3. Add carrots and shallots, Saute for 5 minutes until tender and fragrant.

4. Add your ground beef and season it with salt and pepper, brown until no longer pink.

5. Drain any excess grease.

6. Add tomato sauce, wing, and meat to skillet.

7. Simmer for about 10 minutes over medium-low heat.

8. Stir in cream cheese and simmer until melted.

9. Break each lasagna noodles into 3-4 pieces and stir them into the meat mixture until fully covered in sauce.

10. Lay your noodles flat in the pan.

11. Tuck few slices of fresh cheese underneath and between the noodles.

12. Place remaining slices of fresh mozzarella cheese on top. Bake for about 25 minutes.

13. You have the option to brown your cheese, in that case, you have heat your oven to 425°F and cook for 10 minutes more.

14. Let it sit for a few minutes and top with parmesan and basil.

NUTRITIONAL INFORMATION (PER SERVING):

Calories: 704

Total Fat: 32 g, Saturated Fat: 16 g, Cholesterol: 129 mg, Sodium: 987 mg, Total Carbohydrate: 57 g, Dietary Fiber: 6 g, Total Sugar: 12 g, Protein:43 g, Vitamin D: 1 mcg, Calcium: 544 mg, Iron: 5 mg, Potassium: 1367mg

Braised Sherry Beef Short Ribs

BRAISED
SHERRY
BEEF SHORT
RIBS

PREP TIME: 15 MIN
COOKING TIME: 1 ½ HOURS
SERVING: 6-8

Beef short ribs are already pretty amazing to eat! But most of its magic lies behind how you prepare the dish! This simple recipe will give you the most delicious, mouthwatering and foolproof short ribs! Dark, caramelized and crusty, it'll make you keep coming back for more!

INGREDIENTS:

- 4 bacon slices, cut into ½ inch pieces
- 3 ½ pounds beef short ribs
- Salt and pepper to taste
- 1 bay leaf

- 3 cloves garlic, minced
- 1 onion, diced
- 2 tablespoons all-purpose flour
- 6 sprigs fresh thyme, leaves stripped
- 1 cup dry sherry
- 1-quart beef broth

DIRECTIONS:

1. Pre-heat your oven to a temperature of 350°F.

2. Take a large skillet and place it over medium-high heat.

3. Add bacon and cook for 10 minutes until browned.

4. Transfer crispy bacon to Dutch oven.

5. Keep the bacon drippings in the skillet.

6. Season short ribs with salt and pepper.

7. Heat up bacon drippings in the skillet over high heat and add short ribs, cook for about 3-5 minutes until caramelized.

8. Transfer ribs to Dutch oven (keep drippings in skillet).

9. Add thyme, bay leaf to the skillet.

10. Lower heat to medium and stir in onion, cook for 5-10 minutes until golden.

11. Whisk in flour into onion mix and stir for 1-2 minutes until you have a paste-like texture.

12. Pour sherry into the mixture and cook for 2 minutes.

13. Pour the whole sherry-onion mix into your Dutch oven.

14. Bring the ribs to a simmer and cover your Dutch oven with lid.

15. Transfer oven to your pre-heated oven and cook for about 2 hours until the ribs are fork tender.

16. Remove ribs to your serving platter and keep the sauce in the Dutch oven.

17. Bring the sauce to high heat and boil sauce for 10 minutes until thick.

18. Spoon the reduced sauce over your cooked ribs.

NUTRITIONAL INFORMATION (PER SERVING):

Calories: 439

Total Fat: 19 g, Saturated Fat: 3 g, Cholesterol: 4 mg, Sodium: 740 mg, Total Carbohydrate: 55g, Dietary Fiber: 16 g, Total Sugar: 14 g, Protein: 19g, Vitamin D: 1mcg, Calcium: 296mg, Iron: 8 mg, Potassium: 2192 mg

Fancy Oven-Braised Beef Chuck Stew

BEEF CHUCK STEW

PREP TIME: 30 MIN
COOKING TIME: 1 ¾ HOURS
SERVING: 4-6

Beef is the best meat for stews and braises. Cattle meat can be quite difficult to process and it is important to remember that the way of cooking depends a lot on the meat cuts chosen — of course, we don't make meatballs, rissoles or stews of the meat for steaks or roast beef but use something more suitable.

INGREDIENTS:

- 2 pounds boneless beef chuck, excess fat removed and cut up into 1-inch cubes
- 2 large carrots, peeled and cut into 1-inch pieces
- 2 large celery ribs, chopped into 1-inch pieces
- 1 medium onion, peeled and roughly chopped
- 2 tablespoons tomato paste
- 3 cloves garlic, peeled and mashed
- 1 tablespoon Worcestershire sauce
- 1 pound waxy potatoes
- ¼ cup olive oil
- ½ cup frozen peas, thawed

- 3 cups beef stock
- 1 bay leaf
- 3 tablespoons flour
- ½ teaspoon thyme dried
- ½ teaspoon oregano, dried
- ½ teaspoon black pepper, cracked
- 1 tablespoon fresh parsley, chopped
- Salt to taste

DIRECTIONS:

1. Pre-heat your oven to 300°F.
2. Pat excess moisture from beef using paper towels.
3. Season meat with salt.
4. Take your Dutch oven and heat up olive oil over high heat.
5. Add beef and brown thoroughly on all sides.
6. Once a fine brown texture develops, remove and keep it on the side.
7. Lower heat to medium and add onions, saute for 5 minutes.
8. Add garlic and cook for 1 minute more.
9. Lower heat to medium-low and stir in flour and stir until you have a thin paste.
10. Cook for a few minutes.
11. Pour stock and scrape the bottom to deglaze.
12. Add bay leaf, dried herbs browned beef to your Dutch oven.
13. Add tomato paste, sauce and pepper.
14. Stir and heat It over stove top until it comes to a boil.
15. Cover with tight-fitting lid and transfer to your oven.
16. Braise for 60 minutes.
17. Remove pot from oven to your stovetop.
18. Remove lid and simmer on low heat for 15 minutes until the stew thickens.
19. Stir In peas and chopped parsley.
20. Season with salt.

NUTRITIONAL INFORMATION (PER SERVING):

Calories: 606

Total Fat: 24 g, Saturated Fat: 7 g, Cholesterol: 200 mg, Sodium: 1628 mg, Total Carbohydrate: 23 g, Dietary Fiber: 3 g, Total Sugar: 7 g, Protein:76 g, Vitamin D: 0 mcg, Calcium: 97 mg, Iron: 9 mg, Potassium: 1720mg

Cool Quinoa with **Shredded Beef And Pico De Gallo**

QUINOA
WITH
SHREDDED
BEEF

PREP TIME: 10 MIN
COOKING TIME: 2-3 HOURS
SERVING: 6

This fragrant ginger flavored dish complemented with herbs, cheese and garlic are certainly worth a try!

INGREDIENTS:

- 2 cups cooked quinoa
- 2 pounds medium roasted beef
- 3-4 slices bacon
- 1 cup cheese, shredded
- 1 large tomato, chopped
- 1 large onion, chopped
- 1 large russet potato, cubed

1 turnip, cubed

- ½ small green bell pepper
- ½ Anaheim pepper
- 1 teaspoon ginger, minced
- ¼ jalapeno pepper
- Cilantro, chopped
- 1 tablespoon garlic, chopped
- ¾ cup red wine vinegar
- 1 teaspoon cumin
- ½ teaspoon chili powder

DIRECTIONS:

1. Cut your beef into 1-2 inch cubes.

2. Transfer them to your Dutch oven.

3. Add 2/3 of onion around beef and arrange bacon slices on top of onions.

4. Add minced ginger, red wine vinegar, chopped garlic, cumin, chili powder.

5. Season with salt and pepper according to your taste.

6. Cook on medium for about 1-2 hours until the beef is tender, add potato and turnip once the beef is almost tender.

7. Once tender, remove beef from Dutch oven and shred it well.

8. Remove potato/turnip mixture and leave the liquid.

9. Add cooked quinoa to the bottom of your Dutch oven and spread it evenly.

10. Layer potato/turnip mixture on top of quinoa.

11. Add shredded beef.

12. Sprinkle shredded cheese.

13. Make the pico de gallo by add chopped tomato, pepper, and onion to a bowl and seasoning t with salt and pepper.

14. Carefully place pico de gallo in the center of your dish and garnish with cilantro.

NUTRITIONAL INFORMATION (PER SERVING):

Calories: 601

Total Fat: 19 g, Saturated Fat: 8 g, Cholesterol: 101mg, Sodium: 1745 mg, Total Carbohydrate: 51.5 g, Dietary Fiber: 7 g, Total Sugar: 6 g, Protein:46 g, Vitamin D: 2 mcg, Calcium: 188 mg, Iron: 7 mg, Potassium: 737mg

Meat Roast in Cream White Wine Sauce

MEAT ROAST IN CREAM WHITE WINE SAUCE

COOKING TIME: 2 HOURS
SERVINGS: 4

Fabulously fragrant, tasty, hearty and beautiful, the roast is also very easy to cook! This recipe presents a detailed description of its preparation.

INGREDIENTS:

- 21 ounces boiled potatoes
- 1 tablespoon butter
- 3 ½ ounces bacon (or brisket)
- 1 onion
- 2 garlic cloves

- 1 celery raw, stems
- ½ cup white wine
- ½ cup water
- 1/3 cup cream
- 1 tablespoon cornstarch
- 1 pinch of dried tarragon
- 17 ounces pork

DIRECTIONS:

1. Preheat the oven to 340°F.

2. Fry the chopped meat in your Dutch oven (or brazier) until golden brown.

3. In another pan, fry the sliced bacon or brisket to a crisp crust; remove from pan.

4. In pan used to fry bacon, fry the onions, garlic, and celery until soft.

5. Add bacon and vegetables to the meat.

6. Add wine, water, salt, and pepper; cover and place in oven for 1 hour.

7. Remove from oven; add cream with starch.

8. Stir and heat on the stove to thicken the sauce; add tarragon to taste.

9. Now add the boiled potatoes, and serve!

NUTRITIONAL INFORMATION (PER SERVING)

Calories 323

Total Fat 14.6 g, Saturated Fat 6 g, Cholesterol 39 mg, Sodium 621 mg, Total Carbohydrate 30.8 g, Dietary Fiber 4.4 g, Total Sugars 3.7 g, Protein 12.4 g, Vitamin D 2 mcg, Calcium 39mg, Iron 1 mg, Potassium 856 mg

Pilaf in the Brazier

You can cook pilaf from any meat. This one is cooked from chicken, but you can also choose pork, lamb, or beef.

INGREDIENTS:

- 3 cups rice
- 18 ounces meat
- 5 carrots
- 3 onions
- ½ cup vegetable oil
- seasoning for pilaf (salt and pepper, to taste)

DIRECTIONS:

1. Rinse the rice and soak it for half an hour.

2. Peel the vegetables.

3. Cut the carrots into strips and the onions into rings, and fry in your Dutch oven (or brazier) until half cooked on low heat.

4. Cut the meat into small pieces; add seasoning to taste and fry lightly.

5. Put meat in the bottom of the Dutch oven; pour oil on top.

6. For the next layer, add the fried vegetables, and then the rice.

7. Pour all the ingredients into the water so that the rice is slightly covered. Close the lid.

8. Place in the oven for about an hour.

9. Take it out and mix; serve.

NUTRITIONAL INFORMATION (PER SERVING)

Calories 729

Total Fat 20.6 g, Saturated Fat 4.6 g, Cholesterol 165 mg, Sodium 166 mg, Total Carbohydrate 63.1 g, Dietary Fiber 2.7 g, Total Sugars 3.7 g, Protein 67.7 g, Vitamin D 0 mcg, Calcium 69 mg, Iron 5 mg, Potassium 662 mg

Pork Roast

PORK
ROAST

COOKING TIME: 2 ½ HOURS
SERVING: 4-6

The roast is a dish of pieces of meat, first roasted, and then stewed with seasonings and vegetables. For roast, any meat that can withstand a fairly long cooking, while remaining juicy, will do.

INGREDIENTS:

- 18 ounces of meat
- 2 carrots
- 2 onions
- 2 blue eggplants
- 3 tomatoes
- 3 bell peppers

- 3 garlic cloves
- 18 ounces potato
- 2 cups parmesan cheese, grated
- 1 ½ tablespoons olive oil
- ½ cup butter
- greens and spices to taste

DIRECTIONS:

1. Cut the meat into large pieces and marinate them in spices.

2. Preheat oven to of 360°F.

3. Wash vegetables and peel.

4. Cut carrots into small rings, onion into semi-rings, pepper into straws, eggplants into pieces.

5. Cover tomatoes with boiling water and peel them. Then cut into small slices.

6. Peel potatoes and cut them into large pieces.

7. Lay out all the ingredients in your Dutch oven, pre-greased with butter: potatoes, vegetables, meat. Rotate all the layers several times in a circle.

8. Each layer must be salted and peppered. Cook in preheated oven for about an hour and a half.

9. About 10 minutes before it is ready, remove the roast and sprinkle it on top with grated parmesan cheese and greens.

10. Return to the oven until golden brown.

NUTRITIONAL INFORMATION (PER SERVING)

Calories 534

Total Fat 30.4 g, Saturated Fat 16.9 g, Cholesterol 125 mg, Sodium 568 mg, Total Carbohydrate 30.9 g, Dietary Fiber 5.4 g, Total Sugars 8.9 g, Protein 37.8 g, Vitamin D 11mcg, Calcium 428 mg, Iron 2 mg, Potassium 876 mg

VEGETABLE-FOCUSED RECIPES

Chuck Roast with Balsamic and Dijon

CHUCK ROAST
WITH
BALSAMIC
AND DIJON

PREP TIME: 15 MIN
COOKING TIME: 3 HOURS
SERVING: 5

The savory mustard sauce will add some zesty flavor and pungent hints to tender meat and is sure to conquest even the most fastidious gourmets with its amazing taste. At the same time, this dish is rather simple to cook and won't take much of your time and effort.

INGREDIENTS:

- 4 pounds Chuck roast

- 1 pound small baby potatoes

- 2 bunch of small carrots, tops cut

- 2 cups beef broth
- 5 sprigs thyme
- 1/3 cup balsamic vinegar
- 2-3 tablespoon Dijon mustard
- 1 medium yellow onion, chopped
- 2-3 tablespoon vegetable/ olive oil
- Salt and pepper to taste

DIRECTIONS:

1. Pre-heat your oven to a temperature of 300°F.
2. Heat up your Dutch oven over high heat and add oil, let the oil heat up.
3. Season chuck roast generously with salt and pepper.
4. Add to the pan and brown all sides (2-3 minutes per side).
5. Add chopped onions to the drippings and lower down heat to medium.
6. Add onions and Saute them for 5 minutes until tender.
7. Add vinegar and increase the heat to medium-high.
8. Bring to a boil and keep boiling until the mixture is slightly syrup like.
9. Add Dijon and stir.
10. Add 2 cups beef broth and thyme sprigs.
11. Place lid and transfer to oven, bake for 2 and ½ - 3 hours until it shows a nice tender texture.
12. Add carrots, potatoes to your pot and return to the oven once again.
13. Cook for 30-60 minutes more until they are nice and tender.
14. Season according to your taste and serve.

NUTRITIONAL INFORMATION (PER SERVING):

Calories: 510

Total Fat: 29 g, Saturated Fat: 11 g, Cholesterol: 156 mg, Sodium: 353 mg, Total Carbohydrate: 14 g, Dietary Fiber: 2 g, Total Sugar: 3 g, Protein:46 g, Vitamin D: 0.3 mcg, Calcium: 6 mg, Iron: 30 mg, Potassium: 1197mg

Hearty One-Pot Mushroom Rice

Try cooking rice with mushrooms and garlic! It works out well with white, brown and even wild rice. Actually, the latter really matches mushrooms, fried with butter or vegetable oil.

INGREDIENTS:

- 2 garlic cloves, minced
- 1 tablespoon olive oil
- 1 onion, diced
- 1 pound cremini mushrooms, thinly sliced
- ½ teaspoon dried thyme
- 2 teaspoon Worcestershire sauce
- Salt and pepper to taste
- 1 and ½ cups vegetable broth
- ¾ cup brown rice
- 2 tablespoons fresh chives, chopped
- 2 tablespoons unsalted butter

DIRECTIONS:

1. Take a large sized Dutch oven and place it over medium heat.

2. Add olive oil and let it heat up.

3. Add garlic, onion and cook for 2-3 minutes until translucent.

4. Stir in mushrooms, thyme, and sauce.

5. Cook for about 5-6 minutes until mushrooms are tender.

6. Season with salt and pepper according to your taste.

7. Stir in broth and brown rice.

8. Bring the mix to a boil.

9. Cover and lower down the heat, simmer for 40-45 minutes.

10. Stir in butter and keep stirring it until melted.

11. Serve with a garnish of chives.

12. Enjoy!

NUTRITIONAL INFORMATION (PER SERVING):

Calories: 179

Total Fat: 7.2 g, Saturated Fat: 3 g, Cholesterol: 10 mg, Sodium: 41 mg, Total Carbohydrate: 25 g, Dietary Fiber: 1 g, Total Sugar: 2 g, Protein:5 g, Vitamin D: 0.3 mcg, Calcium: 5 mg, Iron: 25 mg, Potassium: 1200mg

Buckling Greek Veggie Casserole

BUCKLING GREEK VEGGIE CASSEROLE

PREP TIME: 15 MIN
COOKING TIME: 1 ½ HOURS
SERVING: 6

Casseroles come in a variety of forms and variation, but usually in the both US and Europe it is made with the same types of ingredients: pieces of meat, poultry or fish; cut-up vegetables; the base of rice, potatoes or pasta; and some sauce, e.g. meat or vegetable broth, wine, beer, gin, brandy, etc. Another thing that all casseroles have in common: they are usually cooked very slowly and, unlike in most braises, casserole ingredients shall be first fried-up a skillet and then baked in the oven in some kind of Stewpot.

INGREDIENTS:

- ¼ cup feta, crumbled
- 2 tablespoons fresh dill, chopped
- 1 tablespoon oregano, dried
- 1 tablespoon fresh lemon juice
- 4 garlic cloves, sliced

- 1 pound Yukon gold potatoes, cut into 1 inch wedges
- ½ pound green beans, trimmed
- 1 can (14 ounces) whole tomatoes, peeled, quartered with juices

- 1 zucchini, 8 ounces, cut into crosswise into four sections, then cut lengthwise into quarters
- 1 small onion, cut into ½ inch wedges
- 4 tablespoons olive oil, divided
- Salt as needed

DIRECTIONS:

1. Pre-heat your oven to a temperature of 450°F.

2. Take a medium bowl and add onion, zucchini, 1 tablespoon olive oil and toss well.

3. Season with salt.

4. Transfer to a large baking dish and roast for 12-15 minutes until zucchini is about to brown.

5. Transfer zucchini and onion to a wire rack.

6. Add 3 tablespoons oil, green beans, potatoes, tomatoes (with juice), lemon juice, garlic, oregano to another medium bowl and stir, season with salt.

7. Transfer the mix to the same baking dish and top with roasted onion and zucchini.

8. Cover with foil and bake for 30 minutes.

9. Remove foil and stir veggies.

10. Keep baking for about 25-35 minutes more until the potatoes are tender and slightly brown.

11. Sprinkle dill on top and let it sit for about 10 minutes.

12. Garnish and enjoy!

NUTRITIONAL INFORMATION (PER SERVING):

Calories: 163
Total Fat: 11 g, Saturated Fat: 1 g, Cholesterol: 16 mg, Sodium: 214 mg, Total Carbohydrate: 14 g, Dietary Fiber: 3 g, Total Sugar: 4 g, Protein:4 g, Vitamin D: 0 mcg, Calcium: 114mg, Iron: 2 mg, Potassium: 364 mg

Warm Cuddly Winter Minestrone

Minestrone is not just soup. It is a symbol of the Italian dietary approach. Main components of the soup are broth, vegetables, and beans. Italians cook it with seasonal products, but you can still add some frozen peas or beans. A great advantage of this tasty dish is that all of its ingredients are really healthy.

INGREDIENTS:

- 2 tablespoons olive oil
- 1 and ½ cups yellow onions, chopped
- 4 ounces pancetta, diced to ½ inch portions
- 2 cups carrots, diced to ½ inch sizes
- 2 cups celery, diced to ½ inch sizes
- 2 and ½ cups butternut squash, peeled, diced
- 2 teaspoons fresh thyme leaves, chopped
- 1 and ½ tablespoons garlic, minced
- 1 can (26 ounces) tomatoes, diced
- 6-8 cups chicken stock
- 1 bay leaf

- Salt and pepper to taste
- 1 can (15 ounces) cannellini beans, drained and rinsed
- 2 cups cooked pasta, (small sized)
- ½ cup dry white wine
- Garlic bruschetta
- Fresh parmesan cheese
- 9- 10 ounces fresh baby spinach leaves

DIRECTIONS:

1. Place your Dutch oven over medium heat and add 2 tablespoons olive oil.

2. Add pancetta and cook for about 6-8 minutes over medium-low heat.

3. Add onions, celery, carrots, squash, garlic, thyme and cook for 8-10 minutes over medium heat, making sure to keep stirring it from time to time.

4. Once the veggies are tender, add 6 cups stock, 1 tablespoon salt, bay leaf, 1 and ½ teaspoons pepper to your pot.

5. Bring the mix to a boil and lower down the heat.

6. Simmer (uncovered) for 30 minutes.

7. Discard bay leaf.

8. Add beans and cooked pasta, heat it thoroughly.

9. Add more chicken stock.

10. Add spinach and toss the soup with a large spoon.

11. Stir in white wine, pesto and season with your desired amount of salt.

12. Serve with bruschetta on top and a sprinkle of cheese and olive oil drizzle.

NUTRITIONAL INFORMATION (PER SERVING):

Calories: 879

Total Fat: 20 g, Saturated Fat: 5 g, Cholesterol: 110mg, Sodium: 2030 mg, Total Carbohydrate: 132 g, Dietary Fiber: 18 g, Total Sugar: 10 g, Protein:41 g, Vitamin D: 1 mcg, Calcium: 321 mg, Iron: 12 mg, Potassium: 1708 mg

Warm And Slow Cooked Homemade Tomato Sauce

HOMEMADE
TOMATO
SAUCE

PREP TIME: 20 MIN
COOKING TIME: 6 HOURS
SERVING: 6-8

This astonishingly simple yet hearty red tomato sauce is guaranteed to make you forget about all the store bought sauces out there! The simple secret here is to slowly cook the sauce and let the complex flavors form in your Dutch oven. Believe me, the long wait is worth it!

INGREDIENTS:

- 4 cans (28 ounces each), whole tomatoes, peeled
- ¼ cup extra virgin olive oil
- 4 tablespoons butter
- 1 teaspoon red pepper flakes
- 8 cloves garlic, minced
- 1 tablespoon dried oregano
- 1 medium carrot, cut into chunks
- 1 large stem, fresh basil
- 1 medium onion, split in half
- Salt and pepper to taste
- 1 tablespoon fish sauce
- ½ cup fresh parsley, minced

DIRECTIONS:

1. Pre-heat your oven to 300°F.

2. Take a bowl and add tomatoes, crush using your hands and squeeze in your fingers until the pieces are no larger than ½ inch.

3. Transfer 3 cups of crushed tomatoes to a sealed container and keep in the fridge.

4. Place your Dutch oven over medium heat and add olive oil and butter, heat until melts.

5. Add garlic and cook for about 2 minutes until tender.

6. Add pepper flakes, oregano, cook for 1 minute.

7. Add carrot, tomatoes, onion, and basil.

8. Bring to a simmer over high heat.

9. Cover Dutch oven with lid slightly ajar and transfer to your oven.

10. Cook for 5-6 hours until the sauce the mixture is reduced by half and the color becomes deep red, make sure to keep stirring it after every 1-2 hours.

11. Lower temperature if the sauce starts to bubble.

12. Remove from oven using tongs and discard onion halves, basil stems, and carrots.

13. Add reserved tomatoes to the sauce and stir well.

14. Add fish sauce.

15. Season with salt and pepper and stir in minced herbs. Add more olive oil if needed.

NUTRITIONAL INFORMATION (PER SERVING):

Calories: 134

Total Fat: 12 g, Saturated Fat: 5 g, Cholesterol: 5 mg, Sodium: 335 mg, Total Carbohydrate: 6.2 g, Dietary Fiber: 1.4 g, Total Sugar: 2.6 g, Protein:1.2 g, Vitamin D: 4 mcg, Calcium: 36mg, Iron: 1 mg, Potassium: 83 mg

Heartthrob Coconut **Spinach and Chickpeas**

Chickpeas and spinach cooked in a lemon sauce can make a fabulous side dish as well as a worthy main meal.

INGREDIENTS:

- 1 small yellow onion
- 2 teaspoons ghee
- ½ cup sundried tomatoes, chopped
- 4 large cloves, garlic, peeled and minced
- Finely grated zest of 1 large lemon
- 1 tablespoon fresh ginger, peeled and grated
- 1 dried hot pepper

- 1 can (15 ounces) chickpeas, drained and rinsed
- 1 can (13-14 ounces) coconut milk
- 1 pound baby spinach
- 2 tablespoons freshly squeezed lemon juice
- 1 teaspoon ginger, ground
- 1 teaspoon salt

FOR SERVING

- Fresh cilantro
- Whole roasted potatoes
- Toasted unsweetened coconut

DIRECTIONS:

1. Take your Dutch oven and place it over medium-high heat.

2. Add ghee and let it heat up.

3. Add onion and cook for 5 minutes.

4. Add sun-dried tomatoes, fresh ginger, garlic, lemon zest, red pepper and cook for 3 minutes, stirring it well.

5. Add chickpeas, cook over high heat for a few minutes.

6. Add spinach and toss well, make sure to make space using your hand after each addition of spinach.

7. Cook for about 5 minutes until spinach wilts down.

8. Bring to simmer and lower down the heat, cook for 10 minutes.

9. Taste and season accordingly.

10. Add more lemon juice if needed.

11. Serve hot with roasted sweet potatoes, toasted /unsweetened coconut as a garnish.

12. Enjoy!

NUTRITIONAL INFORMATION (PER SERVING):

Calories: 697

Total Fat: 33 g, Saturated Fat: 22 g, Cholesterol: 0 mg, Sodium: 718 mg, Total Carbohydrate: 81 g, Dietary Fiber: 24 g, Total Sugar: 17 g, Protein:27 g, Vitamin D: 0 mcg, Calcium: 266 mg, Iron: 12 mg, Potassium: 2003 mg

Aromatic Cabbage with Mushrooms

From such a seemingly simple and inexpensive vegetable, you can cook truly royal dishes. Stewed cabbage is one of them. Varying spices and additional ingredients, sometimes you get real culinary masterpieces —delicious, hearty, fragrant. Put out the cabbage on the water, with a little oil, or you can put meat, mushrooms, raisins, prunes, tomato paste, beans and other vegetables. In any case, it will be delicious. Try the following, and choose your own favorite recipe.

INGREDIENTS:

- 1 cabbage
- 2 carrots
- 1 onion

- 1 ½ tablespoons vegetable oil
- 2 cups mushrooms
- salt and pepper to taste
- 1 cup marinade

DIRECTIONS:

1. Shred cabbage.

2. Peel the vegetables.

3. Slice the onions into small cubes.

4. Grate the carrots.

5. Cut the mushrooms into small pieces.

6. Place onion, carrots, and mushrooms in a Dutch oven (or brazier), and fry in vegetable oil.

7. Add the shredded cabbage to the vegetables, and fill them with marinade or cucumber pickle.

8. Add spices to taste, cover with a lid, and place in preheated oven for 40 minutes.

NUTRITIONAL INFORMATION (PER SERVING)

Calories 284

Total Fat 12.6 g, Saturated Fat 1.4 g, Cholesterol 0 mg, Sodium 2060 mg, Total Carbohydrate 42.5 g, Dietary Fiber 9.8 g, Total Sugars 24.7 g, Protein 6.1 g, Vitamin D 168mcg, Calcium 143 mg, Iron 3 mg, Potassium 847 mg

DELICIOUS SEAFOOD DISHES

Hunter's Dutch Oven Fish Fry

HUNTER'S
DUTCH
OVEN FISH
FRY

PREP TIME: 10 MIN
COOKING TIME: 10 MIN
SERVING: 6-8

INGREDIENTS:

- 2 cups vegetable oil

- 2 pounds Tilapia fish fillets

- 2 cups dry pancake mix

- 1 and ½ cups flour, in a zip bag

- 2 cups club soda

- 1 tablespoon onion powder

- 1 tablespoons seasoned salt

- Tartar sauce as needed

DIRECTIONS:

1. Cut your fish into 2 inch thick chunks

2. Take your Dutch oven and add oil to about ½ inch depth

3. Pre-heat the oil to 400°F in order to prepare it for frying

4. Add fish pieces to your flour (in zip bag) and shake them well to cover them

5. Transfer floured fish pieces on a paper towel and let it dry for 4-5 minutes

6. Take a bowl and add pancake mix, onion powder, soda, seasoned salt and mix well

7. Add soda until the mixture is just thin enough so that you can pour it

8. Dip fish pieces in the batter and let any excess drip off

9. Transfer them to your Dutch oven and fry for 3 minutes, flip and fry for 3 minutes more

10. Take the fish out once all sides are browned, make sure to check the center of the fish for doneness

11. Serve with your desired amount of tartar sauce and French fries

12. Enjoy!

NUTRITIONAL INFORMATION (PER SERVING):

Calories: 689

Total Fat: 36g, Saturated Fat: 3g, Cholesterol: 49 mg, Sodium: 448 mg, Total Carbohydrate: 64g, Dietary Fiber: 1g, Total Sugar: 1g, Protein: 23g, Vitamin D: 1 mcg, Calcium: 110mg, Iron: 1mg, Potassium: 510mg

Simple and Efficient Oven Seafood Chowder

SIMPLE AND
EFFICIENT
OVEN
SEAFOOD
CHOWDER

PREP TIME: 20 MIN
COOKING TIME: 1 HOUR
SERVING: 4

A big thing for real gourmets from among fish-lovers is properly fried: crispy and crusty fish pieces. By the way, fried fish is better eaten hot, as it can lose most of its nutritional value when cooling down.

INGREDIENTS:

- 1-2 cups milk
- ½ cup butter
- 3-4 cups chicken broth
- 1 cup heavy cream
- ½ teaspoon each, salt and pepper

- ½ teaspoon garlic powder
- 1 potato
- 1 tablespoon each, basil and oregano
- 2 tablespoons paprika
- Scallops, crab/lobster, cod/perch fish
- 2 stalks celery

DIRECTIONS:

1. Place your Dutch oven over medium heat and add butter, let the butter melt.

2. Add onion and celery and Saute them for a few minutes.

3. Add potato and cover with broth.

4. Cook on medium heat until tender.

5. Add basil, paprika, oregano, garlic powder, pepper, salt, and place lid.

6. Cook for 5 minutes.

7. Add fish, crab meat and scallops.

8. Cook until fish becomes flaky.

9. Once the seafood is cooked well, add milk and heavy cream.

10. Stir.

11. Lower down heat and simmer until heated well.

12. Serve with hot rice.

13. Enjoy!

NUTRITIONAL INFORMATION (PER SERVING):

Calories: 293

Total Fat: 21 g, Saturated Fat: 12 g, Cholesterol: 145 mg, Sodium: 562 mg, Total Carbohydrate: 7 g, Dietary Fiber: 1 g, Total Sugar: 2 g, Protein:19 g, Vitamin D: 1 mcg, Calcium: 83 mg, Iron: 2 mg, Potassium: 413mg

Mesmerizing Dutch Oven Salmon Bake

MESMERIZING DUTCH OVEN SALMON BAKE

PREP TIME: 10 MIN
COOKING TIME: 10 MIN
SERVING: 6-8

Braised seafood is a genuine gourmet meal! However, you can still add more flavors and colors to it with vegetables.

INGREDIENTS:

- Tartar sauce
- 1 tablespoon onion powder
- 1 tablespoon seasoned salt
- 2 cups club soda

- 2 cups dry pancake mix
- 2 pounds salmon fish fillets
- 1 and ½ cups flour (in Ziploc)

DIRECTIONS:

1. Cut up your fish into 2-inch chunks.

2. Take your Dutch oven and add oil (a ½ inch deep).

3. Heat up your oil to 400°F, preparing it for frying.

4. Add fish in flour and shake the zip bag well to coat the fish fillets thoroughly.

5. Transfer flour coated fish pieces to a paper towel and dry them for 4-5 minutes.

6. Take a bowl and add pancake mix, onion powder, soda, seasoned salt.

7. Mix well until the batter is thin.

8. Add soda and mix until thin.

9. Dip your floured fish in the batter and let excess dry off.

10. Fry them in the oil for 3 minutes, flip and cook for 3 minutes more.

11. Once the fish is browned on all sides, transfer them to a paper and let them cool.

12. Serve with French fries and tartar sauce.

NUTRITIONAL INFORMATION (PER SERVING):

Calories: 469

Total Fat: 32 g, Saturated Fat: 7 g, Cholesterol: 99 mg, Sodium: 342 mg, Total Carbohydrate: 5g, Dietary Fiber: 1 g, Total Sugar: 0 g, Protein: 38 g, Vitamin D: 0 mcg, Calcium: 125mg, Iron: 1 mg, Potassium: 648 mg

A harmony of fish fillet, onions and tomato sauce provides for a delicious dish with intense taste and nicely balanced flavors.

INGREDIENTS:

- 1 large yellow onion, chopped
- 2 celery ribs, chopped
- Salt and pepper to taste
- 4 large garlic cloves, minced
- Extra virgin olive oil
- ½ teaspoon thyme, dried
- ¾ cup dry white wine
- 1 can (28 ounces) whole peeled plum tomatoes, juiced separated and reserved
- 3 cups vegetable broth
- 2 tablespoons capers
- ¼ cup golden raisins
- 2 pounds sea bass fillet, 1 and ½ inch thick, cut into large cubes (skinless)
- ½ cup fresh parsley, chopped
- Crusty Italian bread for serving
- 3 tablespoons toasted pine nuts, for serving

DIRECTIONS:

1. Take your Dutch oven and place It over medium heat.

2. Add 1 tablespoon of oil and let it heat up.

3. Add onions, salt, pepper, celery and cook for about 4 minutes until tender.

4. Add red pepper flakes, thyme, garlic and cook for 30 seconds until a nice fragrant comes.

5. Stir in white wine and your reserved tomato juice (from a can).

6. Lower heat and bring the mix to a simmer, keep cooking until it is reduced by a half.

7. Add tomatoes, raisins, broth, capers and cook for 15-20 minutes over medium heat until the flavors mix well.

8. Pat fish dry and season it gently with pepper and salt.

9. Transfer the fish pieces into cooking liquid and gently stir until the fish have been covered well.

10. Bring the mix to a simmer and cook for 5 minutes.

11. Remove the Dutch oven from your heat and cover it.

12. Let it sit for about 4-5 minutes to allow the flavors to sip into the fish.

13. Once the fish is flaky, stir in chopped up parsley.

14. Ladle the stew into serving bowls and top with toasted pine nuts.

NUTRITIONAL INFORMATION (PER SERVING):

Calories: 395

Total Fat: 11 g, Saturated Fat: 2 g, Cholesterol: 63 mg, Sodium: 144 mg, Total Carbohydrate: 34 g, Dietary Fiber: 5 g, Total Sugar: 6 g, Protein: 31 g, Vitamin D: 0 mcg, Calcium: 91mg, Iron: 2 mg, Potassium: 899 mg

Fancy Italian Seafood Stew

You can perfectly make fish stew in an oven. It's up to you to choose whether you want to fry it on a skillet first or make it entirely in the oven.

INGREDIENTS:

- 1/2 cup extra virgin olive oil
- 2 celery ribs, finely chopped
- 1 fennel bulb, cored and chopped
- 1 white onion, finely chopped
- 1 tablespoon dried oregano
- Pinch of red pepper, crushed
- 1 and ½ pounds squids, cleaned, bodies cut into ½ inch rings, tentacles halved
- 2 cups dry white wine

- 1 can (28 ounces) tomato puree
- 2 cups water
- Salt and pepper to taste
- 2 lemons, zest of one peeled in strips, zest of other grated
- 1 cup bottled clam broth
- 12 ounces mussels, scrubbed
- 12-ounce littleneck clams, scrubbed
- 12 ounces skinless striped bass fillet, cut into 2 by 1-inch pieces

- 12 ounces shrimp, shelled and deveined
- 2 tablespoons flat leaf parsley, chopped

DIRECTIONS:

1. Add ½ cup olive oil to your Dutch oven and heat it up over medium-high heat.

2. Add celery, fennel, onion, oregano, crushed red pepper and cook for 15 minutes.

3. Add squid and cook over low heat for 15 minutes.

4. Stir in wine and bring to a boil over high heat, cook for 20 minutes.

5. Stir in tomato puree and lemon zest strips.

6. Season with salt and pepper accordingly.

7. Cook on low for 40 minutes until thick.

8. Add water and clam broth, bring to a boil.

9. Remove and discard the lemon zest.

10. Season broth with salt and pepper.

11. Add mussels, shrimp, clams, and cover.

12. Cook for 5 minutes until most shells are open.

13. Add striped bass and cook for 2 minutes.

14. Take a small bowl and add parsley and grated lemon zest.

15. Spoon stew into deep serving soup bowls.

16. Drizzle with a bit oil and serve!

NUTRITIONAL INFORMATION (PER SERVING):

Calories: 626

Total Fat: 25 g, Saturated Fat: 4 g, Cholesterol: 144 mg, Sodium: 2187 mg, Total Carbohydrate: 38 g, Dietary Fiber: 8 g, Total Sugar: 14 g, Protein: 65 g, Vitamin D: 1 mcg, Calcium: 201 mg, Iron: 15 mg, Potassium: 2623 mg

Mexican Seafood Stew

MEXICAN
SEAFOOD
STEW

PREP TIME: 15 MIN
COOKING TIME: 1 HOUR
SERVING: 6

Fruit of the sea recipes has conquered the world with their simplicity in cooking and a reliably nice taste of the dishes. We suggest you cook this braised seafood with vegetables. This is a simple and healthy food that can be served as a side dish or a main meal.

INGREDIENTS:

- 1 pound cleaned squid or 1-1/2 pounds uncleaned
- 1 pound fish fillets
- 1 small yellow onion
- 2 teaspoons ghee

- ½ cup sundried tomatoes, chopped
- 4 large cloves, garlic, peeled and minced
- Finely grated zest of 1 large lemon
- 1 tablespoon fresh ginger, peeled and grated
- 1 dried hot pepper

- 1 can (15 ounces) chickpeas, drained and rinsed
- 1 can (13-14 ounces) coconut milk
- 1 pound baby spinach
- 2 tablespoons freshly squeezed lemon juice
- 1 teaspoon ginger, ground
- 1 teaspoon salt

FOR SERVING

- Fresh cilantro
- Whole roasted potatoes
- Toasted unsweetened coconut

DIRECTIONS:

1. If your squid is frozen, defrost it under dribbling cold water.

2. If the squid has not been cleaned, clean it properly. Grasp head/tentacles firmly in one hand, the body on the other, gently pull the two sections apart.

3. The ink sac and innards will come out from the head, cut the head away and discard everything above the point where the tentacles come together.

4. Go the body cavity, feel for a hard quill, Grasp the body firmly and pull the quill out.

5. Rinse the cavity and tentacles thoroughly and cut the bodies into 1-inch sections.

6. Cut the tentacles in half.

7. Transfer squid to Dutch oven and add 2 quarts water.

8. Add half of onion and half of garlic.

9. Add bay leaves and bring to a simmer.

10. Partially cover the pot and lower heat to keep the liquid in a gentle simmer.

11. Cook for about 25 minutes until the squid is tender.

12. Strain (reserving solids, make sure to discard the bay leaves).

13. Measure out the liquid (should be about 6 cups) and keep it on the side.

14. Wipe the Dutch oven and keep it on the side.

15. Now it's time to prepare your flavored stew base, take your food processor and add remaining onions, garlic, tomatoes and process until smooth.

16. Add oil to your Dutch oven and heat it over medium-high heat.

17. Once hot, add the tomato mixture, stir for 10-12 minutes until darkens.

18. Stir in reserved squid broth and chilies.

19. Season with salt according to your taste.

20. Add potatoes, partially cover and simmer over medium heat for 15 minutes.

21. Peel your shrimp, making sure to leave the final joint and tails in place.

22. Devein the shrimp, making a nice shallow incision down the back.

23. Once the potatoes are cooked and tender, raise the heat a little bit and add fish cubes.

24. Partially cover pot and cook for 3 minutes in a gentle boil.

25. Once the timer runs out, uncover your pot and add back squid and shrimp.

26. Place lid and remove heat, let it sit for 3-4 minutes.

27. Cook for 1 minute.

NUTRITIONAL INFORMATION (PER SERVING):

Calories: 697

Total Fat: 33 g, Saturated Fat: 22 g, Cholesterol: 0 mg, Sodium: 718 mg, Total Carbohydrate: 81 g, Dietary Fiber: 24 g, Total Sugar: 17 g, Protein: 27 g, Vitamin D: 0 mcg, Calcium: 266 mg, Iron: 12 mg

The ingredients are simple, but the result exceeds expectations. This fish can be stewed in the oven or on the stove. It can also be cooked in a multicooker or slow cooker. And the main thing in this recipe is not even the fish, but a carrot component. It is a delicious dish; I know you will love it like I do.

INGREDIENTS:

- 4 hake fish
- 2 onions
- 2 carrots

- 1 bell pepper
- vegetable oil
- salt and pepper, to taste

DIRECTIONS:

1. Preheat oven to 320°F.

2. Cut hake into large pieces, then salt and pepper it.

3. Peel onions and carrots, and remove the bell pepper's core.

4. Cut the carrots into circles, cut the onion into half rings, and straw the bell pepper.

5. First fry vegetables in your Dutch oven (or brazier), then lay the pickled fish on top.

6. Add on top 50 ml (about ¼ cup) of water and put in the oven.

7. Cook for about 20 minutes, then serve.

NUTRITIONAL INFORMATION (PER SERVING)

Calories 255

Total Fat 2.4 g, Saturated Fat 0.5 g, Cholesterol 50 mg, Sodium 284 mg, Total Carbohydrate 13.9 g, Dietary Fiber 3.1 g, Total Sugars 7.1 g, Protein 45.1 g, Vitamin D 4 mcg, Calcium 134mg, Iron 2 mg, Potassium 1068 mg

SWEET & SAVORY DESSERT RECIPES

Supreme Blueberry Cobbler

You can use both fresh and frozen berries, but do let the latter to defrost and remove excess juice. It is important to taste the berries before adding sugar – some of them may be sourer than the others, so you might need a little more sweetener.

INGREDIENTS:

- 2 bags of frozen blueberries
- 1 can cream soda
- 1 box white cake mix
- ¾ cup white sugar
- ½ - 1 cup brown sugar

NUTRITIONAL INFORMATION (PER SERVING):

Calories: 265

Total Fat: 22 g, Saturated Fat: 9 g, Cholesterol: 0mg, Sodium: 80 mg, Total Carbohydrate: 16g, Dietary Fiber: 4 g, Total Sugar: 10 g, Protein: 5 g, Vitamin D: 0 mcg, Calcium: 28 mg, Iron: 0mg, Potassium: 210 mg

DIRECTIONS:

1. Add blueberries to your Dutch oven.

2. Sprinkle white sugar.

3. Sprinkle cake mix on top of berries.

4. Carefully pour cream soda over cake mix.

5. Sprinkle brown sugar.

6. Bake for 30 minutes at 350°F (if using coals, place 15 coals on top and 9 on bottom).

7. Once ready, serve with your desired flavor of ice cream.

8. Enjoy!

Dutch Camping Cobbler Desire

Peach cobbler is a traditional American dish, that has become common in the UK, Ireland, and Canada. This fragrant dessert is similar to a usual pie, but it has no crust at the bottom and is served hot but with an additional cold bonus of an ice-cream scoop.

INGREDIENTS:

- 1 can (14.5 ounces) peaches, sliced
- 1 can (14.5 ounces) fruit cocktail
- 1 can (14.5 ounces) crushed pineapples

- ½ cup Instant Tapioca
- 1 cup brown sugar
- ¼ pound butter
- 1 package cake mix

DIRECTIONS:

1. Line your Dutch oven with foil.

2. Add fruit and tapioca.

3. Sprinkle cake mix evenly on top of the fruit.

4. Add brown sugar and spread them evenly over cake mix.

5. Add butter all over brown sugar.

6. Place lid on your oven.

7. Bake for 45-60 minutes using 6-8 coals on bottom and 14-16 coals on top.

8. Once the cake has absorbed its juice and is no longer dry (with top browned), it is ready.

9. Serve and enjoy!

NUTRITIONAL INFORMATION (PER SERVING):

Calories: 222

Total Fat: 18 g, Saturated Fat: 6 g, Cholesterol: 21 mg, Sodium: 245 mg, Total Carbohydrate: 13 g, Dietary Fiber: 3 g, Total Sugar: 8 g, Protein: 6g, Vitamin D: 0 mcg, Calcium: 172mg, Iron: 1 mg, Potassium: 316 mg

Amazing Triple Chocolate Indulgence

Chocolate will make any dessert even daintier and more tempting. Try making this impossible to resist delicious dark chocolate cake!

INGREDIENTS:

- ¾ bag chocolate chips
- 2 whole eggs
- 1 and ¾ cups milk
- 1 box chocolate instant pudding
- 1 box chocolate cake mix

DIRECTIONS:

1. Line your Dutch oven carefully with aluminum foil.

2. Pre-heat your Dutch oven to high heat.

3. Take a bowl and mix in cake mix, eggs, and milk.

4. Stir well.

5. Stir in pudding and chocolate chips.

6. Pour the mixture into your prepared and pre-heated Dutch oven.

7. Cook for about 40 minutes.

8. Remove the coals from the bottom and keep the top ones, cook for 5-10 minutes more.

9. Once done, serve and enjoy!

NUTRITIONAL INFORMATION (PER SERVING):

Calories: 735

Total Fat: 45 g, Saturated Fat: 27g, Cholesterol: 137 mg, Sodium: 121 mg, Total Carbohydrate: 81 g, Dietary Fiber: 2 g, Total Sugar: 78 g, Protein: 10 g, Vitamin D: 1 mcg, Calcium: 82 mg, Iron: 1 mg, Potassium: 279mg

Exquisite Oven Peach Cobbler

That's a very interesting recipe – something in between a pie and a pudding: gentle, cheerful, pretty and tasty! Cobbler has a distinctly delicate flavor: juicy sweet peach slices melt in the mouth, and the tender juice-soaked dough is almost indistinguishable.

INGREDIENTS:

BASE INGREDIENTS

- 2 cans (16 ounces) sliced peaches, dipped in a syrup of your choice
- 1 pint fresh blueberries
- ½ cup baking mix
- Ground cinnamon
- 1/3 cup sugar

FOR TOPPING

- 2 and ¼ cups baking mix
- ½ cup milk
- ¼ cup butter, melted
- ¼ cup sugar
- ¼ cup cinnamon sugar combined with 2 teaspoons ground cinnamon (mixed)

DIRECTIONS:

1. Pre-heat your Dutch oven to a temperature of 350°F.

2. Grease your Dutch oven with butter, cooking spray or oil.

3. Drain 1 of the peach can.

4. Add both cans of peaches (Drained and undrained) to the Dutch oven.

5. Add blueberries, baking mix, cinnamon sugar and mix well.

6. Make the topping by mixing biscuit mix, butter, sugar, milk in a re-sealable bag.

7. Drop bits of dough and mix well.

8. Use your finger to pour the mixture on top of your peaches.

9. Sprinkle more cinnamon sugar.

10. Place Dutch oven into your pre-heated oven and bake for about 45 minutes.

11. Once the top shows a golden brown texture and is crusty, it is ready!

NUTRITIONAL INFORMATION (PER SERVING):

Calories: 524

Total Fat: 19 g, Saturated Fat: 11 g, Cholesterol: 92 mg, Sodium: 312 mg, Total Carbohydrate: 85 g, Dietary Fiber: 3 g, Total Sugar: 60 g, Protein:6 g, Vitamin D: 0 mcg, Calcium: 27 mg, Iron: 1 mg, Potassium: 285mg

Hearty and Amazing Minty Chocolate Cake

For those of you who like home-made treats we have prepared a delicious and simple chocolate pie recipe

INGREDIENTS:

BASE INGREDIENTS

- 1 box of chocolate cake mix

FOR TOPPING

- 1/4 teaspoon peppermint extract
- 6 tablespoons butter
- 1 and ½ cups milk chocolate chips

FOR FROSTING

- 3 drops green food coloring
- ½ teaspoon peppermint extract
- 2 cups powdered sugar
- 1 tablespoon water
- ½ cup butter, tender

DIRECTIONS:

1. Follow the instructions on your package to prepare the cake batter.

2. Carefully pour the prepared batter into your Dutch oven.

3. Prepare your oven by adding 11 coals on the bottom and 17 coals on the top.

4. Bake for about 25-30 minutes at 350°F, until a toothpick comes out clean from the center.

5. Let it cool.

6. Take a large bowl and add frosting ingredients and whip well until smooth.

7. Spread the mixture over the cooled cake.

8. Prepare the topping by melting chocolate chips and butter in a microwave proof bowl.

9. Stir until the mixture is smooth.

10. Stir in your extract.

11. Spread this mixture over frosting.

12. Let it sit for a while until cooled and cut.

13. Enjoy!

NUTRITIONAL INFORMATION (PER SERVING):

Calories: 482

Total Fat: 30 g, Saturated Fat: 17 g, Cholesterol: 76 mg, Sodium: 224 mg, Total Carbohydrate: 50 g, Dietary Fiber: 2 g, Total Sugar:37 g, Protein:5 g, Vitamin D: 0 mcg, Calcium: 76 mg, Iron: 2 mg, Potassium: 106mg

Traditional Cream Cheese Sheet Cake

It's rather peculiar but still very pleasant and balanced taste. I'd recommend it to everyone who is not afraid of daring combinations and is looking for something special!

INGREDIENTS:

BASE INGREDIENTS

- 1 cup + 2 tablespoons butter
- 2 and ¼ cups sugar
- 2 packs (3 ounces each) cream cheese, tender
- 6 whole eggs
- ¾ teaspoon vanilla extract
- 2 and ¼ cups cake flour

FOR FROSTING

- ½ cup semisweet chocolate chips
- 1/3 cup evaporated milk
- 1 cup sugar
- ½ cup butter

DIRECTIONS:

1. Take a mixing bowl and add cheese, sugar, butter.

2. Mix well to cream the mixture.

3. Add eggs one by one, making sure to keep beating the mixture after every mixture.

4. Beat in vanilla.

5. Add flour and mix well.

6. Grease your Dutch oven with oil or butter and pour the mixture into your oven.

7. Bake for about 30-35 minutes at 325°F.

8. Once a toothpick comes out clean, the cake will be ready.

9. Use 1 and ½ rings on top and 1 ring on the bottom to and let it cool.

10. Prepare the frosting by taking a pan and mixing sugar and milk.

11. Bring the mix to a boil and cover, cook for 3 minutes (don't stir).

12. Stir In chocolate chips, butter and keep stirring until melted.

13. Let it cool.

14. Spread the mixture over your cake.

15. Serve and enjoy!

NUTRITIONAL INFORMATION (PER SERVING):

Calories: 283

Total Fat: 20 g, Saturated Fat: 12 g, Cholesterol: 95 mg, Sodium: 159 mg, Total Carbohydrate: 23 g, Dietary Fiber: 2 g, Total Sugar: 14 g, Protein:5 g, Vitamin D: 0 mcg, Calcium: 64 mg, Iron: 1 mg, Potassium: 151mg

Roasted Apple and Savory Porridge

If you've been looking for an unusual oatmeal recipe, go for this baked porridge with apples and pickled radicchio.

INGREDIENTS:

- 1 and ½ cups white wine vinegar
- 1 and ½ teaspoons fresh ground pepper
- 1 and ¾ teaspoons kosher salt
- 2 medium Chioggia radicchio, chopped
- 5 sprigs parsley + ½ cup extra chopped parsley
- 3 sprigs thyme
- 1 bay leaf
- 2 garlic cloves, peeled
- 4 small shallots, peeled
- 1 cup spelt
- 1 cup sorghum
- 3 ounces prosciutto, thickly sliced
- 3 quarts sodium chicken broth
- 2 pink lady apples, cut into ½ inch wedges
- 2 tablespoons olive oil
- 2 ounces parmesan, grated
- ½ cup heavy cream
- 1 and ½ cups whole milk

DIRECTIONS:

1. Take a medium bowl and whisk in 1 teaspoon of salt, 1 teaspoon of pepper, 1 cup of water.

2. Add radicchio, cover the mixture and let it sit until your dish is ready.

3. Tie parsley sprigs, thyme sprigs, and bay leaf together using a kitchen twine.

4. Add herb bundle, garlic, shallot, sorghum, spelt, broth and about 2 cups water to a large sized pot.

5. Bring the mixture to boil over high heat.

6. Lower down heat to low and simmer for 1 and ½- 2 hours until grains are tender and most of the liquid is gone.

7. Pre-heat your oven to 450°F.

8. Prepare a rimmed baking sheet and line with parchment paper.

9. Arrange speck on a baking sheet and bake for 5-8 minutes until crispy.

10. Let it cool and break it down into medium sized portions.

11. Add apples, oil, ½ teaspoon pepper, ¾ teaspoon salt on another similar prepared rimmed baking sheet and bake apples for 13-15 minutes.

12. Discard the herb bundle from grains.

13. Stir in milk, cream and bring the mix to a boil.

14. Remove heat and blend the mixture using an immersion blender.

15. Once the porridge is thick and creamy, add cheese and keep stirring until melted.

16. Season with more salt and pepper accordingly.

17. Drain radicchio and add them to a medium bowl alongside chopped parsley.

18. Season with salt and pepper.

19. Serve porridge in serving bowls with a topping of roasted apple, speck and pickled radicchio.

NUTRITIONAL INFORMATION (PER SERVING):

Calories: 392

Total Fat: 14 g, Saturated Fat: 4 g, Cholesterol: 10 mg, Sodium: 485 mg, Total Carbohydrate: 59 g, Dietary Fiber: 9 g, Total Sugar: 15 g, Protein: 11 g, Vitamin D: 0 mcg, Calcium: 340mg, Iron: 4 mg, Potassium: 580 mg

Try this excellent fruit dessert for your breakfast! Apples baked in the oven are not only delicious but also good for your health.

INGREDIENTS:

- ½ teaspoon salt
- ¼ cup water

FOR TOPPING

- ¾ cup butter
- ½ teaspoon nutmeg
- ¾ teaspoon cinnamon

- 7-8 large granny smith apples
- ¾ cup brown sugar
- ¾ cup extra sugar

DIRECTIONS:

1. Pre-heat your oven to 350°F.

2. Peel apples and slice them into eighths.

3. Add apples evenly in your Dutch oven and add water over apples.

4. Take your food processor and add topping ingredients, mix them well until you have a sand-like texture.

5. Press topping between your hand to compact it, lay the topping over your apples.

6. Keep repeating until all topping has been used up, making sure to cover all the apples.

7. Cover pan with foil and transfer to your oven, bake for 25 minutes.

8. Remove foil and bake for 10-20 minutes more.

9. Check the tenderness by poking the apples with a fork.

10. Remove your pan from oven and let them cool.

11. Top with ice cream and serve.

12. Enjoy!

NUTRITIONAL INFORMATION (PER SERVING):

Calories: 427

Total Fat: 22 g, Saturated Fat: 11 g, Cholesterol: 41 mg, Sodium: 8 mg, Total Carbohydrate: 58 g, Dietary Fiber: 6 g, Total Sugar: 31 g, Protein: 5 g, Vitamin D: 0 mcg, Calcium: 35 mg, Iron: 2 mg, Potassium: 309mg

FRAGRANT BAKING RECIPES

Simple and Efficient No-Knead Gourmet Bread

Contrary to popular belief, the Dutch oven is actually capable of making amazing baked goods! This sensuously crusty bread with holes is the prime example of the gorgeous baked delicacies that you can make using your Dutch oven!

INGREDIENTS:

- 3 cups all-purpose flour
- 2 teaspoon salt
- 1 teaspoon active dry yeast

- 1 teaspoon fresh rosemary, chopped
- 1 and 2/3 cups warm water (at 110°F)
- 1 teaspoon fresh sage, chopped
- 1 teaspoon fresh thyme, chopped

DIRECTIONS:

1. Add flour, salt, and yeast in a large sized bowl. Mix well.

2. Add water and herbs and mix again until incorporated.

3. Cover the bowl with plastic wrap and let it sit for 18-24 hours.

4. Flour and prepared your workspace.

5. Once the dough has risen, transfer dough to your workplace and dust with flour.

6. Fold dough in half and form a nice ball, stretching and tucking the edges methodically.

7. Flour a kitchen towel and place the dough ball on your floured towel.

8. Cover with another towel.

9. Let the dough rise for 2 hours more.

10. Transfer a lidded Dutch oven to your oven, let it pre-heat.

11. Remove hot Dutch oven from oven and remove the lid.

12. Carefully turn the dough ball into your Dutch oven (seam side up).

13. Shake the dough to ensure that it is distributed evenly.

14. Cover with lid and bake for 30 minutes.

15. Remove lid and bake for 15-20 minutes more.

16. Remove loaf from the dish and let it cool.

NUTRITIONAL INFORMATION (PER SERVING):

Calories: 350

Total Fat: 3 g, Saturated Fat: 1 g, Cholesterol: 1 mg, Sodium: 240 mg, Total Carbohydrate: 67g, Dietary Fiber: 3 g, Total Sugar: 1g, Protein: 12 g, Vitamin D: 0 mcg, Calcium: 26mg, Iron: 4 mg, Potassium: 120 mg

Extremely Satisfying Dutch Oven Pizza

EXTREMELY SATISFYING DUTCH OVEN PIZZA

PREP TIME: 30 MIN
COOKING TIME: 30 MIN
SERVING: 3

If you like both pizza and mushrooms, go ahead to merge them in one dish and make some mushroom pizza. Trust me, it turns out really fabulous, and the recipe is quite simple!

INGREDIENTS:

FOR PIZZA DOUGH

- 4 and ½ cups bread flour
- 1 tablespoon salt
- ½ tablespoon granulated sugar
- 1 envelope (7g) instant dry yeast
- 15 ounces lukewarm water

- 3 tablespoons olive oil, more for brushing

FOR PIZZA SAUCE

- fresh ground black pepper
- pinch of granulated sugar
- 2 teaspoons olive oil
- 2 clove garlic, grated

- 1 teaspoon salt
- 1 can (15 ounces) tomatoes, drained

TOPPINGS

- 8-10 ounces whole mozzarella, sliced up into ½ inch cubes
- Toppings such as olives, prosciutto, mushrooms etc.
- Fresh basil, chopped
- Fresh parmesan, grated

DIRECTIONS:
FOR DOUGH

1. Take a bowl and use an electric mixer (fitted with paddle attachment) and whisk flour, salt, yeast, and sugar.

2. Add olive oil, water, and mix until fully incorporated (try using the hook attachment).

3. Keep mixing the dough until it becomes smooth, take it out and transfer to a lightly floured surface.

4. Keep kneading by hand for a few minutes.

5. Divide the dough into three equal pieces (about 12-13 ounces each) and form balls.

6. Transfer to a baking tray and lightly brush with olive oil.

7. Cover with plastic wrap and transfer to a warm spot.

8. Let it rise for 1 ½ hours.

FOR SAUCE

1. Take your blender jar and add drained tomatoes, puree.

2. Transfer the pureed tomatoes to a bowl.

3. Stir in grated garlic, olive oil, salt, sugar, pepper.

4. Keep it on the side and let it refrigerated until needed.

MAKING PIZZA

1. Pre-heat your oven to 450°F, keeping your Dutch oven on the lowest part of the oven.

2. One the dough has doubled in size, roll dough on a lightly floured surface and roll it out into a disk of 12 inches wide.

3. Once the dough does not bounce back anymore, let it rest for a while.

4. Transfer prepared the dough to a piece of parchment paper and let it rest for a few minutes.

5. Lightly brush dough with olive oil.

6. Spread a third of your sauce in a thin layer.

7. Top with your desired toppings.

8. Take a small paddle and bring pizza to your Dutch oven.

9. Bake for 12-15 minutes until the crust shows a golden texture and the cheese melts.

10. Remove the Dutch oven from oven and use parchment paper to carefully lift out the pizza to your cutting board.

11. Slice and enjoy!

12. Repeat for the remaining pizzas!

NUTRITIONAL INFORMATION (PER SERVING):

Calories: 851

Total Fat: 37 g, Saturated Fat: 15 g, Cholesterol: 78 mg, Sodium: 965 mg, Total Carbohydrate: 93 g, Dietary Fiber: 5 g, Total Sugar: 4 g, Protein:35 g, Vitamin D: 0 mcg, Calcium: 559 mg, Iron: 6 mg, Potassium: 409mg

KITCHEN TOOLS

Mixer

This little helper is something every person should have in their kitchen. It is a very handy kitchen tool, as it does the heaviest work – kneading the dough. **Within 5 minutes you can have super pliable and soft dough,** and keep your energy for something else. When making pizza, you have to knead your dough at least 10 minutes to activate the gluten and make the dough elastic. But if you have a mixer with a hook attachment, you can focus on making the sauce and leave the dough up to this genius helper. This kitchen tool is great to use for any type of dough, including heavier pastries.

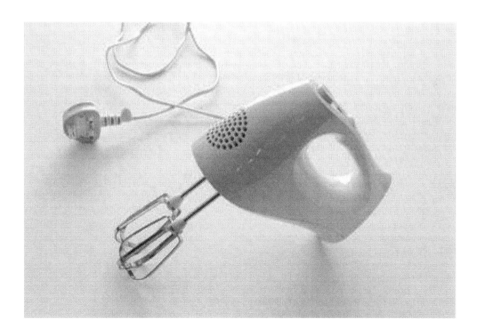

Food Processor

A famous motor-driven kitchen appliance to cook food. Unlike blenders, the food requires a particular amount of liquid to move particle around its blade. It is good for **kneading and mixing doughs, pureeing, grating cheese or shredding and grinding items**.

Oven

An oven is essential for drying, baking or heating of meat, batter, dough, and vegetables. You can use it for heating, roasting, and baking.

Cheese Grater

Pizza is a delicious dish, and we all would agree it would not be the same without cheese on it. Cheese is a staple ingredient for pizza making, and when speaking about the cheese, it cannot be used in large slices on the pizza. **To get your cheese perfectly grated, use stainless-steel cheese graters.** They will perfectly grate the cheese and make it properly prepared for use on pizza. Besides grating the cheese, you can grate some other ingredients as well, like salami or bell peppers.

COOKING MEASUREMENT CONVERSION

US Dry Volume Measurements

1/16 teaspoon	a dash
1/8 teaspoon	a pinch
3 teaspoons	1 tablespoon
¼ cup	4 tablespoons
1/3 cup	5 tablespoons + 1 teaspoon
½ cup	8 tablespoons
¾ cup	12 tablespoons
1 cup	16 tablespoons
1 pound	16 ounces

US Liquid Volume Measurements

8 fluid ounces	1 cup
1 pint = 2 cups	16 fluid ounces
1 quart = 2 pints	4 cups
1 gallon = 4 quarts	16 cups

GROCERY SHOPPING LIST

FLOURS & GRAINS

- [ ] All-Purpose Flour
- [ ] Cake Flour
- [ ] Bread Flour
- [ ] Pancake Mix
- [ ] Cake Mix
- [ ] Baking Mix
- [ ] Instant Tapioca
- [ ] Spelt
- [ ] Yeast
- [ ] Crumbs
- [ ] Gnocchi
- [ ] Lasagna Noodles
- [ ] Pasta
- [ ] Bruschetta
- [ ] Rice
- [ ] Quinoa
- [ ] Sorghum
- [ ] Corn Starch
- [ ] Soda

OILS, VINEGAR, & CONDIMENTS

- [ ] Extra-virgin Olive Oil
- [ ] Soy Sauce
- [ ] Tomato Basil Sauce
- [ ] Worcestershire Sauce
- [ ] Fish Sauce
- [ ] Tartar Sauce
- [ ] Tomato Paste
- [ ] Red Wine Vinegar
- [ ] Balsamic Vinegar
- [ ] Marinade
- [ ] Peppermint Extract
- [ ] Mustard
- [ ] Vanilla
- [ ] Kosher Salt
- [ ] Sugar

MEAT

- [ ] Chicken
- [ ] Bacon
- [ ] Pork
- [ ] Beef
- [ ] Chuck Roast
- [ ] Pancetta

FRUITS

- [ ] Apples
- [ ] Coconut
- [ ] Blueberry
- [ ] Peach
- [ ] Fruit Cocktail

DAIRY

- [ ] Yogurt
- [ ] Milk
- [ ] Coconut Milk
- [ ] Butter
- [ ] Ghee
- [ ] Heavy Cream
- [ ] Whipping Cream
- [ ] Mozarella
- [ ] Parmesan
- [ ] Feta
- [ ] Cheddar
- [ ] Cream Cheese
- [ ] Eggs

SEAFOOD

- [ ] Tilapia
- [ ] Scallops
- [ ] Crab
- [ ] Salmon
- [ ] Sea Bass
- [ ] Squid
- [ ] Mussels
- [ ] Clams
- [ ] Shrimp
- [ ] Hake Fish

VEGETABLES

- [ ] Mushrooms
- [ ] Onion
- [ ] Carrots
- [ ] Celery
- [ ] Bell Pepper
- [ ] Tomatoes
- [ ] Zucchini
- [ ] Potato
- [ ] Scallions
- [ ] Kidney Beans
- [ ] Peas
- [ ] Turnip
- [ ] Eggplant
- [ ] Cabbage
- [ ] Olives, canned

SEASONINGS

- [ ] Garlic
- [ ] Cinnamon
- [ ] Pepper
- [ ] Spinach
- [ ] Lemon
- [ ] Thyme
- [ ] Rosemary
- [ ] Nutmeg
- [ ] Cumin
- [ ] Paprika
- [ ] Tarragon
- [ ] Parsley
- [ ] Garam Masala
- [ ] Sage
- [ ] Cilantro
- [ ] Shallots
- [ ] Turmeric
- [ ] Curry
- [ ] Chives
- [ ] Fennel
- [ ] Coriander

SWEETS

- [ ] Chocolate Chips
- [ ] Chocolate Instant Pudding
- [ ] Chocolate Cake Mix

DRIED HERBS & SPICES

- [ ] Oregano
- [ ] Rosemary
- [ ] Bay Leaf
- [ ] Ginger
- [ ] Lemon Pepper
- [ ] Ground Mustard
- [ ] Chili
- [ ] Red Pepper Flakes

NUTS & SEEDS

- [ ] Raisings
- [ ] Jalapenos
- [ ] Butternut Squash
- [ ] Chickpeas
- [ ] Pine Nuts

BEVERAGES

- [ ] Dry Red Wine
- [ ] White Wine
- [ ] Sprite
- [ ] Sherry
- [ ] Cream Soda
- [ ] Chicken Broth
- [ ] Beef Stock
- [ ] Clam Broth
- [ ] Vegetable Broth

FROM THE AUTHOR

I am a **professional chef**, and one of my favorite hobbies is hiking. In the winter, when backpacking with kids gets difficult, we enjoy nice family dinners, gathering around the table and recalling our summer adventures and delicious meals that we cooked at the campfire.

Of course, I try my best to make something to remind my loved ones of those times. Frankly speaking, **I really enjoy cooking in a Dutch oven**, particularly because one meal is enough to **make the whole family happy.**

I have different Dutch ovens to cook with at home versus when camping. Either way, though, I encourage the kids to help me, and we make up some amazing dishes together!

Let me invite you to the world of heartwarming dinners with savory meals cooked in a Dutch oven.

OUR RECOMMENDATIONS

RECIPE INDEX

Copyright

Made in the USA
San Bernardino, CA
29 March 2019